DON'T QUIT YOUR DAY JOB

DON'T QUIT YOUR DAY JOB

▼

ADVENTURES FOR THE WORKING STIFF

Jay H. Toberman

Writers Club Press
San Jose New York Lincoln Shanghai

Don't Quit Your Day Job
Adventures For The Working Stiff

Writers Club Press
an imprint of iUniverse.com, Inc.

For information address:
iUniverse.com, Inc.
5220 S 16th, Ste. 200
Lincoln, NE 68512
www.iuniverse.com

ISBN: 0-595-13820-9

Printed in the United States of America

To My First Traveling Companion
and the Guy Who Started Me On My Adventures
Don Thompson Jr.

Do You See The Circle In My Beer?

CONTENTS

INTRODUCTION

Once again it was happening. Not all of a sudden, but gradually. That's how they all started, gradually. The urge, the feeling, the wanting. It had been five years since I started contemplating these far off thoughts. I guess I was too occupied these last five years to have these feelings, these feelings of adventure. I was just a working stiff in the corporate world. However, I knew it was time for an adventure.

I guess my feeling for adventure started without my even knowing it. I didn't even know I thrived for adventure. Usually, the thriving for adventure comes around age thirty-five. You reach this age and have the feeling that life is passing you by. You picture yourself as some Indiana Jones person. Then you wake up.

I left home at 18 to attend college. Most of my high school buddies went to the local university and lived at home. I went away to school, lived on campus, and stayed on campus on weekends, not going home. That may have been the start of it. The need to do something different. The need to be adventurous.

The real test came one summer day. I was doing accounting work for a small company. My college buddy came up to me and asked if I wanted to take a trip. I asked where to? He said Montreal, Canada. Living in Minneapolis, Minnesota, Montreal was about 1,500 miles away. He said we'll be gone two weeks. I had to see if I could get the time off. I asked how we would get to Montreal. My buddy said we would hitchhike. Hitchhike? Hitchhike! I thought, you peon, we'll take my car. He didn't say anything-I started thinking. I had not done any real adventures. I was only twenty-one. It could be fun.

That was the start of it. That was the start of my adventures for the working stiff, one little line on a clear summer day, casual conversation. Do you want to take a trip? Easy as that. From that, I became an adventurer. Small scale, weekend wanderlust. No way would I climb the highest mountain. No way would I even be a great adventurer. Just a working stiff breaking the pattern of everyday life.

My adventures would take me onto five continents. All modes of transportation such as a plane, train, automobile, canoe, raft, backpack, and thumb. My adventures would cost me a chance at marriage, find me broke, and almost cause me to lose my life. I've almost died or felt like dying from altitude sickness, hypothermia, heat exhaustion, and dysentery.

Extreme headaches and weakness crossing the autoplano in Peru, freezing, shivering on the mountains of Kilimanjaro in Tanzania and Mt. Kinabalu in Borneo. Heat exhaustion in the Darien Gap. I just wanted to lay there and let the leaf ants take me away. Constantly, trying to find a bano in Mexico. Hell, I might even have died from a stop in a Chaing Mai brothel in northern Thailand, but that's another story.

Knowing all this, knowing how I loved and lost, gone broke and almost died, I knew it was time, time for another challenge. Time to get the old body in shape. Time to start planning, time to start researching, time to wonder what the hell I'm doing this for. However, I knew the positives far outweighed the times of being unpleasant. I knew it was time for an adventure for the working stiff.

My reasons for doing an adventure is the thrill of the unknown. I've always wanted to see other lands, learn about other cultures, and meet new people. All of this happens in my travels. Adventure travel doesn't mean you have to go through a miserable time to call a trip an adventure. You don't need to encounter mishaps to make the trip exciting. I didn't need to get heat stroke, miss planes, suffer acute hypothermia, or anything else to have an adventure. Just being there, anywhere different, is the adventure.

How To Choose An Adventure: Where, Why, and How

There is a whole world to choose from of where you can travel to. To help narrow it down, ask yourself these questions. How much time do I have? Being a working stiff, the best I could hope for is two weeks away from work. Even though I currently have four weeks vacation, I can only take two weeks in a row. I may try for three in a row. How will I get to where I'm going? That helps to narrow it down. Where does Northwest Airlines go? Doing a lot of business travel on my job, I was able to collect frequent flyer miles. Therefore, the destination would be Europe, Asia, or Australia.

How would I get around once I got to where I was going? Previously, not wanting to spend the time to research a trip, I relied on adventure travel companies. Adventure travel outfitters are for the person who wants adventure, yet wants the itinerary planned. I was never disappointed. I spent a lot of time learning what each offered. I looked for the one that could give me the best adventure at the lowest cost. By lower cost, you camp more, stay at no-star hotels, and eat a lot of rice. If you want more luxury, an adventure outfitter will find you a trip staying in good hotels with restaurant meals. However, be aware of what you are getting. In looking at a two-week trek through the jungle of the Darien Gap, one trip operator was almost $1,000 more than the other. I asked why their price was so high. The reply was we stayed in better hotels. I answered, "Hotels? It's a jungle! There aren't any hotels! Do you have air-conditioned tents?" Then they said that their trip leaders were very knowledgeable. It sounded more like choosing a pair of designer jeans. I went with the cheaper outfit and had a great time.

The expansion of a multitude of Internet sites can help with the decision of where, why and how. Testimonials, shared experiences displayed on Internet sites can give you personal experiences of what other travelers have encountered. Regard these experiences as information only. Travelers are not the same. Some may like to see museums while others like late night activities and just hanging around doing much of nothing.

The gathering of information will be time consuming but make it fun. Planning an adventure and thinking about it is part of the fun and excitement of an adventure trip. Not having happen what you had planned on your trip is just part of the adventure. You'll learn to test yourself at compromise, disappointments, exciting happenings of non-planned events that only an adventure trip can provide. In the following chapters, I will show you different aspects of adventure travel by my encounters. Remember, I am not a travel expert. I did these trips just to do something different. After all, I'm really just an everyday working stiff. I'm not ready to quit my job, sell my house, sell my kids, put everything in storage and go. No, instead I will keep my job, lead an everyday life and be happy knowing, thinking of what adventure lies ahead.

CHAPTER 1

▼

HITCHHIKING/HOSTELS: ADVENTURE VS. SAFETY

I would not recommend this type of travel. It was the best way at a low cost. Back in earlier years, you didn't have as many nuts on the road. Canada even promoted hitchhiking through commercials on picking up Canada's youth. A youth hostel system spread from Nova Scotia to Vancouver. Maps were available of hostel destinations like road maps showing rest stops. At the University of Ottawa, you got a bunk in the co-ed gymnasium, fruit cocktail, ride into downtown Ottawa and back. In the morning, coffee, bus ride taking hikers east on Highway 1, coming back to get and drop off in different spots, hitchhikers going west on Highway 1, all for one dollar. One buck. If you didn't have a dollar, you swept floors. What a great way to see a country. We got rides from a girl who wore "Yes" earrings, and told us her parents were out of town, hippie van with a joint being passed around, having to join in to keep the ride going, guy getting married the next day driving like a maniac as my friend and I fought for a pillow in the back seat. A business man complaining about mice eating his bagels who bought us lunch, hopping in the back of a manure truck and ending up at a junction in the middle of nowhere, rolling down a hill and spending a glorious night under the stars to squeezing into a family car with members on a vacation only to break down due to all the weight. However, the most memorable was by an elderly couple, Garth and Gurly Brown. We had left Ottawa that morning and rides were scarce. Only traveled about 100 miles. It was late afternoon when Garth and Gurly drove up and offered us a ride. They were only going about 20 miles to their home in Deep River. It was about five in the afternoon when we arrived. Garth told us that there weren't any hostels in the town and offered to put us up for the evening. I looked at my friend, we didn't want to impose, we told them we didn't get far that day, (not that we had any place to get to) and three hours of daylight left for another possible ride. Dropped off. Out came the thumbs. No slacking off for us. We waited and waited. It was seven-thirty when Garth and Gurly came by. They were going shopping and again offered us a place for the night. My friend and I looked at each other again, felt uncomfortable about going with them. Not out of fear, just didn't want to impose. We again declined. They gave us their phone number. It was now eight-thirty, it was getting dark, it was getting cold. I was coming down with a cold. My friend turned to me and said "You make the call."

Garth picked us up and brought us to their home, where they made us something to eat. We shared in Garth's home made brew. Finally, had a shower and a bed to sleep in. Morning came with a big breakfast and a ride to the town's outskirts. I wrote down their address and sent them a thank you note after the trip.

In Japan, drivers who picked up hitchhikers received awards with a coupon system. A traveler would most likely get asked over for dinner.

The only reason I hitchhiked is I didn't even think that I shouldn't. Plus, there were two of us. I also learned that there is an art to hitchhiking. You have to work for your ride. You can't just lay lifeless along the road with your thumb out. Needed is a stand up position, no smoking, a destination sign, and a sincere eye contact with the driver as he or she goes by. Since my buddy towered over me, we had an act. Being that hitchhiking to Montreal was such a blast, the following year we made it out to Banff National Park by way of thumb. Our last time hitchhiking was in Europe. We weren't as successful as cars were smaller and rides generally harder to come by. We decided to go by train after one ride with a man who sped down a hill telling us this was his first time driving since his eye operation. One kid picked us up in Germany and offered us a place to crash for the night. We refused, but gave him our address in the states should he ever get over to Minnesota, naturally one in a million chance. Phone rings one night, couldn't believe it. That kid in Germany was student teaching at a suburban school next to us.

After traveling with my old college buddy for six summers which included two summers hitchhiking in Canada, one in Europe, two car camping adventures to Canada and the Northern U.S. and one stupid, idiotic car camping trip to Mexico City, he got married.

I owe a lot to Don Thompson, Jr. He got me started on the adventurous life I was to lead. One thing I was blessed with is having a traveling companion, a friend that made the trips fun and exciting. We were complete opposites, from different backgrounds. Yet we were the best of friends and best traveling companions. We were going to write in his marriage vows when he says he takes thee Virginia to be his wife, except for two weeks each summer when he takes thee Jay on an adventure trip. From that point, I knew I lost a traveling companion. I then started researching worldwide adventures.

There are many adventurous benefits to hitchhiking/hostels. One is you never know where you might be spending the night. If rides are good, you'll go far. If rides are poor, you may spend the night in the same place you slept the previous night. Flexibility, with no timetable is an essential part of hitchhiking.

While living in Florida, I picked up a hitchhiker as I was turning onto Hwy. 95 from Miami. I asked him where he was going. He pulled out a map and in trying English said, "Dania." Here was a guy from France, about my age of twenty four, seeing the United States by way of hitchhiking. He wanted to get to a campground in the city of Dania, just south of Ft. Lauderdale. Since Dania was on my way home, I drove him to the campground. The campground was a pit. I could see the disappointment in my foreign passenger's eyes. What do I do now? How would I feel if the roles were reversed? I would be in a foreign country and didn't like or know where to stay. Therefore, I couldn't just drop him off. I didn't speak French and he didn't know English. I couldn't ask him what he wanted to do. All I knew was here was a foreigner having an adventure, meeting with a stumbling block. We left the campground. I managed to let him know I was taking him to my apartment. Once we got to my place, I called the University and asked for the French Department. Upon reaching a French speaking teacher, I told her what was going on. I needed an interpreter to see what I could do and what the Frenchman wanted to do.

His English name was Jim. Jim was traveling the States going now to Atlanta, on up to Detroit and from there to Canada where he had friends he was to meet up with. The conversations resulted in Jim staying overnight in my apartment. Jim and I had a great time trying to converse. I showed him around the area and was as hospitable as I would want to be treated if I was in his situation. As I dropped him off on the highway the next day, we hugged our farewells. I thought how nice it was to be able to assist someone on their adventure. We exchanged addresses and who knows. Maybe one day.

That's the excitement of hitchhiking. Jim's plan was to get to the state park in Dania. He nor I had any idea our lives would interface for a couple of days. When Don and I were hitchhiking, we had not planned to be invited to an elderly couples home for their hospitality and to spend the night. With hitchhiking, there may not be any timetable to keep or any destination to get to on time. There is not too much to worry about.

Where ever the rider ends up for the evening is where the rider will be. Hitchhikers may benefit from nice, unexpected happenings from their drivers. That's the excitement and adventure of hitchhiking.

Understand, that this type of adventure can go south very fast. A ride could be a cause for trouble. If possible, hitchhike on a busy entrance ramp of a highway. Refuse a ride if you feel uncomfortable with who is in the car. A simple, no thanks, to the driver is all that is needed as you walk away, behind the car.

As I said at the beginning, I would not recommend this type of adventure travel in today's world. Some countries may be safer than others. I never worried about safety. Of course, Don was six feet four. If you're going to hitchhike, try to do it in twos. It saddens me that I can not recommend this type of travel when I enjoyed it so much and had wonderful experiences from traveling by way of the thumb.

CHAPTER 2

▼

EAST AFRICA ADVENTURE: TRAVEL COMPANIES

Gathering adventure catalogs was fun. Reading about exotic adventures was just that, reading. Would I actually go? The travel companies wanted you to buy their adventures. The descriptions were very entertaining and exciting. All kinds of places to travel to, all kinds of prices. "Once you have heard the roar of a lion at close quarters in the wild, once you have watched the ambling herd of elephant with trotting calves progressing across the grasslands of East Africa, the two dimensionally of caged animals, and their captors strikes you hard" (Encounter Overland, 1992). I chose a 30-day East Africa overlanding trip. I wanted to see my favorite Tarzan movies up close and in person. This would be my second cross-continent trip as I spent six weeks in Europe with Don six years prior to this. East Africa would be my first major trip on my own. There are many differences between adventure tour companies. Just look in the back of magazines such as Outside, Backpacker, Explore, and such to find the directories of advertisements from tour operators. The ads are saying, choose me, choose me. Write or call to have a catalog of their trips sent to you. You will be amazed at the colorful catalogs they send out. Glossy photographs of far away destinations. Descriptive adventures to get your juices and imagination running in overdrive. You will be overwhelmed with the choices and the experiences you can challenge yourself to. The hard part will be which one to choose. That's where the narrowing down part takes place.

First ask yourself what are your abilities. Will you look for an easy going, moderate, or rigorous adventure? If you're afraid of water, jungle river rafting may not be your first choice. Do you get winded climbing a flight of stairs? If your answer is yes, you will need to work yourself into shape if your wanting is to climb Mt. Kilimanjaro. Maybe you have an active bladder which could rule out a rock climbing adventure.

How much money are you able to allow for an adventure trip? The costliest item of most adventures is getting to and from the starting point. Do you want pampering or a challenge? Do you need a four star hotel or would you be willing to stay in a no star hotel, a hovel, or a tent. Maybe a grass hut with no running water. Under the open sky with just a rain tarp over your head.

Are meals included in the price or is there a food kitty? I don't care for a food kitty. A food kitty is where, for each meal, a collection is made. Problems can arise when some want a gourmet meal and others don't. You can see where uneasiness can set in. Choose the trip with the food included in the cost of the trip unless you are in a city and meals are on your own.

Who does the menu planning? Who does the food shopping? Who does the cooking? This will depend on the type of trip you sign up for and a difference in cost between travel outfitters. If a cook is provided, the meals are planned, the food bought and prepared while you are out exploring for the day. On my trip to Africa, we divided into groups. For the day, one group would plan the menu, get the money from the driver, shop the markets and cook the meal. Another group would set up the camp while the third group did the dishes. Even though being on the cooking team takes time, it gives you the experience of shopping the local markets and getting a feel for the local flavor. If you are on a long overland adventure, these chores are necessary. Of course, on the Africa trip, I was on baggage detail each day. Alan and I loaded and unloaded the luggage each day so I was never on the cooking detail. Naturally, if most meals will be in restaurants, cost of a trip will be higher.

I chose to travel with Adventure Center in California who were agents for an English outfit named Encounter Overland. My main reason was price, along with the full gambit of what the trip included. Serengeti Plains, Ngorongoro Crater, Lake Manyara, and a climb up Mt. Kilimanjaro.

Another reason for lower cost was the lousy room service. There wasn't any as most of the nights were spent camping. Not at some lodge, but out in the bush. This seemed more adventurous. My planning of the trip started. It seemed this trip and future trips started out the same way. I would tell people, start saying that I was going to East Africa. Naturally, they all thought I was nuts. The more I talked about going, the more excited I became. Soon, I told enough people that I had to go. I couldn't back out. So it began. I was going to East Africa. I was to meet my fellow travelers at some hotel in Dar Es Salaam. A lot of preparation went into the planning and tasks. I started to jog to get into condition. I had to get a visa. I had to get 9 shots, which was the worst, as I wasn't good with needles. Traveling to a third world country required a certificate of vaccination. Shots for tetanus, cholera, yellow fever, smallpox, diphtheria, and who knows what the others were for.

I go in for the first set of shots. I'm standing up as I'm getting poked for small pox. Then I get a shot for something else. I'm getting light headed. I said I need to sit down, so I sit. Next thing I know I'm catching Z's on the floor. I couldn't believe it. My childhood fear of shots got the better of me. It was quite comical.

The day finally came to leave. I would fly to New York, catch a plane to London, then onto Dar Es Salaam after a day in London. The adventure started earlier than I wanted. I arrived in London at seven-thirty in the morning. I am unable to sleep on an airplane, so I was going to a hotel and sleep upon arrival. I knew I should try and stay awake to avoid jet lag. I thought a couple of hours wouldn't hurt. However, I had a bigger problem than wanting to go to sleep, My luggage. I waited for my luggage. I'm still waiting for my luggage. No luggage. This was not good. I talked to an airline agent who found my luggage, in New York. No problem. They would deliver my luggage to me the next day. "What hotel will you be at?" they asked. Calmly, I said, "hotel?" "Yes, what hotel will you be in so we can deliver your luggage?" I explained that I would not be in a hotel tomorrow. I'll be somewhere in Dar Es Salaam in Tanzania. I am only in London for the night. The luggage found its way to me that night in London. What a relief.

I walked around London that day, stopped in at Encounter Overland, the tour operator I was traveling with. I received a T-shirt that said, "Where there's a wheel, there's a way". Nothing too exciting as I was having jet lag. I went back to the hotel, my luggage had arrived, so I went to sleep.

No problems leaving Heathrow, British Airways down to Dar Es Salaam, capital city of Tanzania. Upon arriving at the airport, one fills out a form stating why you are there, the money you have, when you are leaving, where you will be staying. Not knowing how to lie and cheat yet, I wrote camping in the place that I would be staying.

Handing over my passport to immigration, the officer looked over my form and said, "camping not allowed, where are you staying?"

"Ah…um, you see, ah…"

"Camping not allowed, where are you staying?

"Ah, I am with a group, we're camping in…"

"Camping not allowed, find out where staying." He handed my form back, kept my passport and sent me back on my way. I saw a trip companion filling out the form. In place of where staying, he put Post Resante. So, hell, I put Post Resante and got back into line. Officer stamped my form, passport, and let me through. Afterwards, I asked where is it that I am staying? It was the post office. I had learned that you write in or tell officers what they want to hear. Camping wasn't allowed, but having the general post office as an address was acceptable. Therefore, by putting on the form something that was acceptable was all that was needed.

I found my way to the hotel where the group was to meet, an international gathering for sure. England, Switzerland, Germany, Ireland, Belgium, Australia, and Zambia were represented. With such a mixture of cultures and personalities along with being in a faraway place, I was in for a real adventure.

There was an evening pre-trip meeting. We got to know each other in the group and learned what we would be responsible for. The group leader mentioned if you used drugs, to please stay behind. No one could help you if caught, not the American Embassy, or whatever embassy, no one. I was to room or tent with Paul from Germany. This would not be popular as Paul was the first one up in the morning, and with a boastful voice said, "Gud moning, evreyone, time to get up, time to get up." Pretty soon shoes were being tossed at him to quiet down.

This was to be an overlanding trip. Overlanding is riding in the back of a Bedford truck. Individual seats, cooking stove and a button. The button was to notify the driver to pull over for a "rest stop". Our first heading was to Lake Manyara. The going was very slow, as the roads were just long stretches of dirt and gravel. Nothing up ahead but the open road. No McDonalds or Holiday Inn signs. We were heading into the back country. When it started to get dark, we pulled off to the side of the road to set up camp along with the lions, elephants and other local inhabitants. No such thing as an organized camp ground anywhere. The truck carried tankers of water for cooking and washing. The bushes were the bathroom. You learn very quickly that modesty goes out the window. Open A-Frame tents with mosquito netting was our home. The first night I didn't get any sleep as I kept reaching in my sleeping bag and throwing out creepy crawling what-evers. I'm glad it was dark and I couldn't see what was crawling around. The mosquitoes were bad but only on this night.

In the morning, two gun toting soldiers were in our camp. There was a war going on with Idi Amin of Uganda at the time but that was further away. Here we were out in no where and these two are standing here. We just went about our morning as they just stood and watched. I still walked between something or someone and the soldiers just in case.

We headed to the steep slopes of the Great Rift Valley to arrive at Lake Manyara. Millions of flamingoes make the lake a deep pink. Pelicans, marabou stork and crane also thrive here. Watching a stork standing alone in the water, a pair of eyes from a pink bald head with floppy ears appeared. The stork looked like lunch for the hippo that was rising out of the water. As lazy and slow as a hippo may seem, it is best not to disturb one. Mean and relatively fast, they would not hesitate to take a bite out of you. From here we headed towards Kili-Mount Kilimanjaro. We stayed at a base camp to Mount Kilimanjaro. It would be a five day trek. Three days up, two down. Our goal was to hike to Gilman's Point, altitude 18,480 feet, and from there to Uharu Peak at 19,340 feet where we would be at the top of Africa.

We put a change of clothing in a bag. Porters would carry the food and gear. This would not be a technical climb but one to be cautious about because of the high altitudes we would reach. We all started off together, weather was beautiful. Sun shining. Temperature in the 80's. We would soon break up as some would walk faster, while others stopped to photo-graph the lush surroundings. I was in the jungle with its hanging vines. I was just waiting to hear the chant of Tarzan. We climbed through forests and grasslands to Mandara Hut at 9,000 feet. Here we would spend the night to acclimatize. A-frame hut had tables on first level, bunks on upper level. Using the outhouse was the most dangerous part of the trip. Upon opening the big door, you grab a bar on the doors other side, and hold on for dear life. There is a big hole that leads to an abyss that you don't want to fall in to. You squat, do your thing, and get the hell out of there. This was not a place to do your crossword puzzles. Time for dinner. This should be interesting. Dinner was a bowl of oxtail soup, bread, sardines, and bananas. This is why I lose weight on these trips. At least they are good for something.

The next day we made a sharp climb to Podocardus Hill, then easy going over moorlands of rock and flowers. We were into the clouds as we reached Horombo hut at 12,300 feet. Altitude sickness was setting in on a couple of hikers. You get the worst headache you can imagine, become weak and sick. The cure is to lay still 24 to 48 hours while you acclimate or go back to a lesser altitude. They headed back down. Fog started setting in, cold and rain followed.

Day three was harder going as the altitude increased. Exposed reaches of sand and volcanic dust as we crossed the saddle between Mawenzi and Kibo Peaks. I was with two girls and one guy as we had lost track of the rest of the group. Rain turned to snow. What started in eighty degree weather was now in the mid-thirties. We were still in shorts. There was no shelter, no trees, barren. We were soaked when we saw Kibo Hut up ahead. We had reached 15,300 feet. One of the girls started throwing up. I was shivering as companions from the hut rushed down to assist us the rest of the way. Shivering. Was hypothermia setting in? Hypothermia is the lowering of one's body temperature. Different stages from incoherence to death. To get warm, one may need to be body to body, skin to skin to get the other person's body heat up. They took off my drenched clothes and stuck me in a sleeping bag. When they asked me if they should put the English girl Hazel in the sleeping bag with me to get my body heat from, saw me smile, they knew I was all right.

It was hard to get warm. The only wood brought up was to cook with. We were over 15,000 feet. There wasn't anything outside the hut. Light snow was coming down.

The next challenge was to reach the top. A start at 1:30am was necessary to reach the first summit at sunrise. The climb would be steep and hard going over the last 1,000 feet to Gilman's Point to see a view worth every step. Then another 1.5 hours around the lip of the crater to Uhuru Peak at 19,340 feet. In reaching the top of Africa, you stop every 20 steps to catch your breath. However, you can't stop to rest for long, as it is too cold to stop. It turned out I would not have to worry about this. My shoes were too wet. I wasn't prepared enough. Out of the eighteen of us, five did the climb. Unfortunately, there was too much cloud cover to see the vistas. I knew that it still would have been worth it to get to the top.

Stepping out of the hut the next morning felt like stepping on the moon. Just barren land and rock. The descent to Horombo hut was quick and easy by comparison. Lush greenery was coming into view as we reached the lower altitudes on the way to our base camp. Looking back at Kili, we could see the fresh snowfall. There are not other peaks to detract from it's immensity. There it sits in solitary majesty rising from the surrounding plains as a monument to the geologist forces which shaped Africa.

Next stop was the Ngorongoro Crater. We spent Christmas Eve at a camp atop the crater. We ate a decent meal that night, steak. Zebra steak. I couldn't tell if the stripes across the meat were from the grill or the skin of the animal.

We sat around a fire, girl played a guitar as we sang Christmas carols. I stared into the fire, thinking of where I was, half way around the world, sitting in a bush, waiting to get attacked by a band of monkeys, starving as I couldn't eat this so called food, rushing around the darkness to find an unoccupied bush. What the hell was I doing here? Then I thought, I would not want to be anywhere else.

The next day we split up into jeeps to descend into the crater. The crater is the most concentrated area for animals. Twelve miles across and almost sheer-sided, the Ngorongoro Crater is a sheltered haven for wildlife. Zebra, wildebeest, rhino, and buffalo graze the Crater floor while lion, leopard, and hyena shelter and watch beneath the trees and along lakes. You could almost reach out and pet a lioness as they lazed around under a tree. That's what they wanted you to think. Come and pet us, we won't bite. Then lunge and you become lunch. We stayed in the confines of the jeep. What a treat to see National Geographic up close and personal.

Next stop, the Serengeti plains. A sea of grasslands and home to the great wildebeest herds, gazelle, giraffe, and animals I never heard of like Topai and Geerenuk. We were even able to see the rare cheetah with her cubs. Also the much-poached rhino. I was constantly in awe. The night sounds were spectacular. The hunters and the hunted, who would make it through the night? Flying high in the sky. Lurking from a tree branch waiting for an animal to drop, the dreaded vulture awaits it's next meal. Up ahead a hyena collapses. The vultures sweep down from the sky. Gathering and flaying away at each other they start ripping apart the fallen hyena. A jackal tries sneaking in, only to be scolded away. The fighting, the tearing, and eating of the hyena. At the end, only a skeleton.

A stop in Nairobi, Kenya and Sam's hotel. Time for a modern city and some tourist shopping. Going back across the border into Tanzania was not easy. Seems there was a selfish border war between the two countries. It seemed tourists flew into Nairobi, stayed in Nairobi hotels, shopped Nairobi stores, and ate in Nairobi restaurants. Tourists would cross into Tanzania to see the Ngorongoro crater and the Serengeti plains. However, these would just be day trips and then right back into Kenya to spend the tourist dollar. Therefore, we were not allowed to cross the border into Tanzania. We needed to get through to get to Dar Es Salaam to catch our flight home. No go. We had a next day hard drive to get to another crossing. Still trouble. After about an hour, cigarettes, bottle of liquor and a couple hundred bucks, we got through. Hustled down to Dar Es Salaam where I caught a plane to London with the rest of the group.

Jessica, one of the girls, invited me to her home in Cambridge. I took the train up, saw the countryside, Oxford, and enjoyed a nice after-trip get together. Over twenty years later, I still share holiday letters with one of the travelers, Steve Andrews. The camaraderie with this group was something to cherish.

CHAPTER 3

▼

FLORIDA EVERGLADES: WHEN THE ELEMENTS SAY NO

It was getting to be about a year since my East Africa journey. It was time to do another adventure. Funds did not allow me to do an overseas adventure. The current Minnesota winter did not allow me to do camping. I don't winter camp. So how do I go camping in the winter? I go to Florida. I also needed to do more than just go to Florida. I needed an adventure. I rounded up my cousin, Vic. We decided to canoe the wilderness waterways through the Everglades. This was not going to be all that easy. I wrote to the Chamber of Commerce and the Forest Service. I checked out materials at the library and went to the local travel bookstore. I found out that the wilderness trail was 99 miles from Everglades City to Flamingo. A leisurely pace would make it a seven day trip. The problem was once we got down to Flamingo, how would we get back? A shuttle was out of the question, as it was 300 miles from Everglades City to Flamingo by road. Catching a float plane to take us back would be too expensive. What to do? By studying the maps, we would start at Everglades City, canoe down to the Broad River which connected out to the Gulf of Mexico, canoe up the Gulf towards Ten Thousand Islands and back to Everglades City. Sounded easy enough. Since we were going on the Gulf of Mexico, we would need charts, nautical charts. This would be a lot more different than any little Minnesota river trail map. We would need to know about tides, as I found out later.

The best months for Everglades canoeing is November through February. Less bugs, less rain. South enough in Florida where warm temperatures should prevail. This type of trip can be a great adventure and if you have camping equipment, cost can be minimal. We decided to rent the canoe and paddles from an outfitter. We would load up my car with equipment and buy most of the food once we reached Florida. It was fun gathering the information and planning the trip. The trip would only be a week plus the drive there and back. Any one can do the trip and there are many, many canoe adventures one can plan. I was limited in my choices since it was winter. Vic was a terrific traveling companion. We were looking forward to the adventure. You don't have to go to a foreign country or to some jungle to have an adventure. You can make your own adventure right in your own area at very low cost.

The day came to head out. Loaded up the car and headed southeast. We knew we would be spending Christmas and New Year's in the Everglades. What better place to spend the holidays? We arrived in Everglades City. Registered at the forest ranger station. Told him of our plan. Received equipment from the outfitter. An old aluminum canoe. It would be hot and uncomfortable. However, we would be crossing some large bays and a fiberglass canoe would be harder to control.

The adventure started off from Chokolaskee Point on a nice, hot sunny day. The day couldn't have been more ideal. After paddling about three hours and getting stuck on an oyster bed, we set up at Lopez camp site. So much for limited bugs that the winter season would have. Mosquitoes galore. I have never been in such a horde of buzzing. We couldn't even sit around, they were so bad. The ranger came by and said this was the worst camp site for mosquitoes. We crawled into the tent about seven as we couldn't even cook a meal. Just ate some snacks, read and played cards. We went to sleep about eight and listened to the sounds of the night. I swear, something was right outside our tent. Spooky it was. An orchestra of buzzing. Just a constant humming. Panic set in when I had to go to the bathroom. I had to get fully dressed including putting my mosquito head dress on. Rushed outside. Not an easy chore. However, it's nice to be a guy at emergency times like this.

The next morning was still so buggy out, we just had a can of juice and a buttered bagel and got the hell out. It was a cloudy day with a light rain. The wind picked up a bit. Crossing Sunday, Oyster, and Hudson Bays were slow with the strong wind blowing. The Everglades are a big mangrove swamp. Mangroves have roots growing above the water. It was so thick that we couldn't even pull over to rest. Vic was dragging his fishing line when he got it snagged or so he thought. As he reeled it up, a small pompano was on his line. Still paddling away, our butts were getting sore. We were headed to Watson Place campground. This was the homestead of the old bootlegger. Thought it would be an interesting place to spend the night. We never got there. We were sore and tired. Wind picking up and water getting rougher. All of a sudden, out of nowhere, we spotted a house of some sort. We started heading towards it. As we got closer, we noticed a dock and steps heading up to a small shack. We were sore from sitting and paddling for 3 1/2 hours. Therefore, we were going to rest on the dock. We didn't know if anyone was home. We didn't notice any movements. Looked deserted. We pulled up and discovered a vacant bunk house. What a treat. It was Christmas and what a better present to get. Our own little cabin. 3 bunk beds, table and chair with an old kitchen sink. We had a bed, mattress and pillow to sleep on. We brought in our gear and made ourselves at home. It was great. No bugs. Warm breeze. Our Christmas dinner consisted of chow mien. Wind started blowing harder. A cold front was moving in. The temperature got down to 40 degrees. We went to bed but it was hard to sleep as the wind was rattling the cottage.

We woke up to a cold morning. Had a good breakfast of cheesy scrambled eggs, toasted bagel, juice and hot coffee. The day was clear and it was starting to warm up. We decided to stay at our little paradise. We were catching rays on the roof when we found out what this place was. Laying on the roof with the only care being when to roll over, we heard a motor boat. Before we knew it, the boat docked and up the steps came a group of five. They were in the cabin. We were on the roof scurrying down. We came upon the owner, Cecil. Cecil was a fishing guide. This was his noon time stop to use the bathroom, clean the morning catch and have some lunch.

He didn't mind us there as long as we cleaned up. Sometimes he arrived and some party-goers had messed up the place and even had some fire damage. We assured him we would take care with our stay. We said our good-byes and climbed back on the roof. What a great day. Sunshine all day, warm perfect night. Another night with no bugs, a mattress and pillow.

It was now the fourth day. We set off early. The weather started off cool but warmed up. We went down Alligator Creek which is just as I pictured the Everglades to be. Long, narrow passageway. Heading for a campsite, we rounded a bend on Plate Creek. There on the creek bank was an alligator basking in the sun. Al became startled when he heard and saw us. He slithered on into the water. I was just waiting for him to upend our canoe and have us for lunch! Upon arriving at Lostman's Five Bay campsite, we noticed it was full. Looked like a bunch of fisherman, drinking fisherman. We headed to a campsite at Onion Key. We ran into an oops: oops, we shouldn't have come. Campsite was closed for restoration. A decision had to be made. It was getting dark. We would not be able to make another campsite. I am a "leave no trace" camper, so we set up shop. We cooked on the camp stove rather than make a fire. During the night, something was getting into the garbage. I went out to check. Flashlight in one hand, canoe paddle and a knife in the other. Whatever it was, ran up a tree as I approached. It wasn't a raccoon.

Now it was our fifth day out. It was freezing this morning so we just packed up and left without eating. We passed a ranger who said it was forty degrees out. The paddling was hard as we crossed a windy and wavy Big Lostman's Bay. It was a real chore paddling. Reaching the Broad River we went upstream to get to Camp Lonesome Mound. Passed another alligator and many egrets, herons and cormorants. There were other campers at this site. Two couples from Massachusetts. Nice to enjoy some other company as we exchanged camping stories. Got to bed at 9 PM. Checked a weather report from a radio to find out forecast and tide. We were to head out to the Gulf of Mexico the next day.

On day six, we started off by heading out the Broad River which connected to the Gulf. Stopped at the Broad River campsite where the previous nights campers, Doug and Pat had reached. The waterway out to the Gulf was rough and we were all deciding whether we could make it on the Gulf to the next campsite with such a wind blowing. Doug and Pat had a motor for their canoe and thought they could make it. After they left, we gave it a try. Made it to the Gulf at low tide. We could camp out on the beach as we saw someone doing or we could paddle out three miles to deeper waters. We tried reaching the beach, but it was low tide. The bottom was a soft mud so we couldn't get there. We would have to paddle out to deeper water or go back to Broad River campsite. Going back to the campsite would be a waste so we fought the wind and waves for three hours just to get around the sand bar and up the beach a way. I discovered a new canoe stroke called the stationary stroke. Paddle, paddle, paddle, and get nowhere. Finally, high tide. As the water came in, we headed up Highland Beach. It was too late to make it to Lostman's Key. So we camped out on the beach. The high wind almost blew our tent away. For dinner, we just munched. Cracked open the bottle of champagne that we were saving for New Year's Eve.

What a beautiful morning day seven started out to be. Nice and calm. When we woke at six, it was still dark. We needed to get out while tide was high. We made it to Turkey Key campsite by eleven. It was like a tropical paradise. A little island with sand beaches. We set up camp, caught afternoon rays and read. Not a care in the world. In the evening, we just sat along the water and gazed up at the clear sky full of stars. I knew I would sleep well tonight.

On this eighth and final day, we woke up early again to catch the high tide. The trouble was the wind was blowing so hard, we could not leave. Stranded, we walked to another part of the island where the wind was not blowing on us and caught rays. Took a quick dip in the water. Cold but felt good. Now we wondered how we were going to get out of here. It's too hard to canoe in the Gulf of Mexico on a windy day. Our water supply was low. It was New Year's Eve. Crawled in early since we drank the champagne the night before. We were attacked by some small animal during the night. Something jumped on the tent and tried to get in. We kept scaring it away. We had to get out the next day.

The next day, our ninth, started out with clear and calm weather. We got another early start. Heading back to the starting point at Everglades City. We saw a bald eagle. As we paddled, a trio of dolphins swam along side. They seemed to smile as us and say, follow us as they swam away. Stopped at a key (island) in the Ten Thousand Island area. We came across Doug and Pat. It was good to see them again. Their dog Billy was happy to see us. We chit-chatted a while, caught rays and headed back to base. Got a motel room. I always do this after a camping trip so I can partake in the three "S's (shit, shower, shave). We had a festive dinner at the Captain's Table consisting of prime rib and wine. It was great. I went to bed at eleven. Still woke up at six the next day.

CHAPTER 4

▼

PERU: LOST LUGGAGE AND THIRD WORLD AIRLINES

Hidden among the bleak Codilleras, where the Andes thrust up their highest peaks over folds of valley and plateau, lies the turquoise jewel of Lake Titicaca, and the stark remains of the Inca Empire.

Huge stone fortresses, temples and arches lie scattered and forgotten along the hilltops, and hidden in the mists and silence is Machu Picchu, the last Inca stronghold and one of the Eight Wonders of the World.

It was a couple years after the Everglades trip that I was getting the fever. The fever of adventure. I had spent the past couple of summers running a canoe program at a summer camp in the Adirondacks. What a fun way to spend a summer. I was barely eeking out a living selling real estate and here I was leaving for the summer to go to camp. Now I was looking to go on another adventure. This scarcity of funds would narrow my search for an adventure. Since I couldn't afford to go to the other side of the world, I would only go part way. Therefore, South America was the

choice and narrowing it further, looking at all the adventure travel catalogs, comparing prices and times, Peru was the destination. Overlanding
for 30 days from Lima around the country and back to Lima was the trip.

Time for the vaccinations. Shots. I went back to the clinic with my
international certification of vaccinations in hand. The nurse said to me,
"I remember you." I realized it was the same nurse who gave me the shots
when I went to Africa. The same one who asked me how I was after I had
fainted from my first set of shots. Feeling kind of embarrassed, I said in a
Stan Laurel way, "I'm better now." I was. I was not afraid of the needle any
more.

The day came to leave. Everything was a go and I headed toward the
airport. I checked my bag and was on my way. I was on American Airlines
to Dallas where I would transfer to Miami. Disaster struck right away. The
flight to Miami was delayed in Dallas/Fort Worth for 1 1/2 hours. I made
it to Miami at one in the morning. The plane to Lima was leaving in a half
hour. I had to get my suitcase. It wasn't there. Time was running out. I had
to catch Aero Peru. I was in a pickle. I had met a friend of my brother's on
the plane from home. Dan knew of my predicament. I couldn't wait anymore. I ran to catch my next plane. I would worry about getting my suitcase when I got to Lima. Made it to the gate with no time to spare. They
had already shut the doors. I was escorted down the jetway and on to the
plane.

I arrived in Lima at six in the morning. I had to get some help to get my
suitcase. I had taken American Airlines to Miami and Aero Peru to Lima.
When someone arrived at the Aero Peru counter, problems. Me Espanol es
no muy bueno. They didn't understand that I needed to contact American
Airlines to send my suitcase on the next Aero Peru flight. I went over to
Eastern Airlines as I found an English speaking agent. She asked if I had
flown Eastern. I said no. She said I should have and could not help me. So
much for customer service. No wonder they went bankrupt. Back to Aero
Peru where an English speaking agent said for me to see Senor Herrera.
After an hour search, I found Senor Herrera. I told him of my dilemma.

He shuffled through some papers, came upon a slip, and told me my suitcase would arrive at seven on the next morning's Aero Peru flight. Dan Witkowski saved the day. He found my suitcase in Miami and put it on the next Aero Peru flight.

My trip was leaving Monday. I would get my suitcase on Sunday and everything would work out. I met a girl, Radjie, at the airport. She was traveling on her own. It was nice to find another English speaking person. We teamed up for the day and got a room at night. A real dive at the Hotel Richmond. No water, toilets didn't flush, noise from the outside. I couldn't sleep. What could I expect for 165 soles ($1.65). We walked around Lima.

The next morning, I took a cab to the airport. The plane was to come in at seven. The plane was delayed until eight. At eight, the plane was delayed now to eleven but not confirmed. I was told to call back to check. The plane had not left Miami. It may not leave at all. I took a cab back to the Hotel Richmond. I told Radjie, I'm going to Residential Santa Rosa where the Encounter Overland group was to meet. I met the group. I had a breakfast of cheese omelets and orange juice for 240 soles. I called the airport. Flight confirmed to arrive at a quarter past twelve. I took a bus to the airport.

I looked for Senor Herrera. No one knew him. Nobody knew English. My Spanish was not good enough to help me. Through Spanglish, I explained that my luggage was on the plane. Then I saw my suitcase. Due to customs, it was a bit of a hassle, but I got it. I headed back to the Santa Rosa Hotel where E.C. was paying for tonight's room. I finally took a shower and put on clean clothes.

We had a pre-departure meeting. Leader said that if anyone had a need to use drugs to please stay behind. Nothing, nobody, nada, can help if you get caught. You won't get out if caught. We went to dinner which was great. Loin steak, potatoes, salad, wine. Too much to eat. Z's at eleven.

Finally on my third day, we started off. We stopped at a market in Lima to shop for food. We headed out from Lima to Cerro Azui. This area is all desert. Lots of shacks for housing. Camped in the desert next to the Pacific Ocean. We went swimming, then a dinner of chili and rice. Out in this nowhere land of sand, we came across a peasants restaurant. Really strange to see out here with nothing around. Sat around with group and learned of other's horror stories of trying to get to Lima with canceled flights and broken down planes. As always, the camaraderie is one of the highlights of these trips. There are no rest rooms out in the desert. You have to walk to a sand dune to hide behind and dig a hole. One gal started walking and walking. She turned to look over her shoulder at the "group". We yelled out "we can still see you".

The fourth day was a travel day. Down to Paracas by way of the Pan American highway. Just a long highway through a desert. Stopped and shopped, then to the beach. Camped next to a motel, so we had a chance to shower. The Swedish girl, Simone, invited me for a drink. I had the native Peruvian drink-a pisco sour.

On our fifth day out we took a boat out to Ballestas Island. The island is a wildlife refuge for sea lions, penguins, and thousands of birds. On the way out to the island, we passed a candelabra shape in the sand. Nobody knows how it got there or why. There are plans to construct a natural history museum here since it is one of the best marine reserves in the world. The area here has been developed as a resort with a beautiful bay but deadly jelly fish to beware of if one goes swimming.

We stopped at a museum in ICA with a collection of ancient engraved stones and mummies. Camping out next to a motel in Nazca. A quick dip in the pool, dinner and beers.

What a treat we had in store the next day. I was in a 4-seater plane which flew us up and over an amazing site. The Nazca lines. You cannot see the shapes from the ground as they are so vast that you need to be up in a plane. No one can explain how these lines and shapes got there. Myths such as a calendar, tribal heritage symbols, to markings from visitors from out of space. Shapes, forms such as a spider, bird, condor, monkey, spaceman appeared over this vast desert area. It was really weird.

From Nazca, we headed to the deserted town of Tanaca. All kinds of homes and buildings which were now abandoned, looked like a wealthy community once. The city had a motel overlooking the Pacific, a school, a jail, strongly built homes of brick and adobe with thatched bamboo roofs. Time for dinner in which we had beef stew followed by a camp fire with driver Tony going over the continuing route and me with a couple of camp stories.

The seventh day was another travel day. Nothing terribly exciting. Just desert scenery.

On the eighth day, we arrived in Arequipa. We decided to go shopping around town. We had to take team turns with guard duty around the truck. I bought a hat for 1000 soles as I sweetly smiled and pinched the women's cheek who was asking 1200 soles.

We set up camp outside of town. We met another Encounter Overland group who were doing a sixteen-week tour of South America. Camped with them tonight. I tried to buy film, but the price was 11,000 soles ($12). Stories galore from each group's happenings.

Trouble, life threatening trouble on our ninth day out. We were driving over the Autoplano. When we got up to 15,500 feet, we came across a stranded bus. The bus had a flat tire. We stopped to help as he didn't have a jack. However, this wasn't his only problem. His spare was flat. Someone else had gone for help so we left. Then it hit me. Out of nowhere. I had stepped off our truck to walk around. Being all of a sudden at an altitude of 15,500 feet and not acclimating, it hit me like a ton of rocks. Pounding headache, weakness, and dizziness. I couldn't even walk. Altitude sickness. Nothing would help except waiting it out for 24 to 48 hours while my body adjusted to the altitude or get to a lower altitude. My tent-mate Brian from Australia, set up the tent. Others had to do my chores. I literally crawled to the bathroom area. I went to sleep at 6PM. At about midnight, I woke and was feeling a bit better. However, Brian was in a poor way. He was almost crying. His heart was pounding so hard, he thought it was going to bust. I made it to our guide who said there was nothing to do but relax and wait till morning. Back at the tent, Brian was scared. I told him I would sit up with him. This lasted about 3 minutes, as I was getting weak again. I said to Brian, I'll see you in the morning, as I was fading fast. There I was in the Andes Mountains and I couldn't enjoy the scenery.

I woke up on what was now the tenth day feeling shitty. We left from Tincopolca heading to Juliaca. I was not able to eat. We stopped in Santa Lucia where we were surrounded by curious children. As soon as the cameras came out, they scattered. This town does not see foreigners too often. I was feeling better. I was starting to rally. In Juliaca, we went to an Alpaca market. What bargains. Double knit Alpaca sweaters for 10,000 ($11). Wall hangings from $6.00.

Day eleven started with a drive to Puno. Then we took a boat ride out to the Uros Islands on Lake Titicaca. These are Reed Islands that people live on. You sink as you walk on the ground. It's too bad these islands have become very touristy. Their way of life now centers on the tourists.

The Indians who live here charge for having their picture taken. These islands are made of reeds which grow in Lake Titicaca. As the old reeds rot away under water, new layers are added on the surface. It's always interesting to me to see how others live. Being out on an island, fish is the main diet. Back in Puno, we had lunch and shopped.

The next day after spending a second night camped outside of Julicia, we loaded up on supplies for the long day's drive. Roads are poor. With speeds at 15 MPH on traveling days such as this day, not much happens. You read, write in your journal, stop for lunch, play cards. Nothing too exciting. You just have to remember where you are. At a place so remote from the usual everyday humdrum back home, that a traveling day is no big deal. It is not a wasted day.

On the road again the next day. We came across a hot sulfur spring with a cold station running next to it separated by a little island. Finally a hot bath. Driving, camping for a few days with no real bathing chances. This was going to be a treat. The trouble was our swimsuits were packed in the luggage, which was packed in the truck which wasn't accessible. One has to remember that when you are on these trips, modesty goes out the door. Your inhibitions need to be left at home. So it's the girls upstream, the guys downstream and into the water. You need to get clean. What a great feeling, sitting in that water. A real refresher. Back on the road we passed farm fields all day and noticed the farmers using methods from Inca times. They were holding onto a plow pulled by oxen. We found a clump of trees, a river, and set up camp.

It was our fourteenth day on which happened to be Christmas Eve Day. We arrived in Cuzco. Very crowded. All the farmers came from their villages for market and Christmas. We had a free day in which I walked the narrow side streets. We camped at the Saxaramon ruins which overlooked the city of Cuzco. What a sight with the town lit up including the cathedral. Breathtaking. I almost went to midnight mass. Almost. Big chicken and rice dinner for our evening meal.

Christmas day was a do anything you want day. Slept till nine. Stayed around camp. Read, relaxed. What a place to spend Christmas. Past Christmases, I've spent camping on the Ngorongoro Crater in Tanzania, camping in the Florida Everglades, and now camping on Inca ruins in Peru.

I helped with dinner. Baked fresh bread, chicken, steak, and leg of lamb. A bunch of locals just watched us all day. A soccer match started between the locals and us along with the goats, chickens, cows, and pigs that were roaming around. A cow made for a good goalie but the pigs wouldn't take a pass.

Day after Christmas was a lot of fun. We went to the Pisac market. I bought myself a beautiful wall hanging along with smaller wall hangings and pillow coverings for gifts. Hiked the Pisac ruins. Spectacular sight that my pictures won't do justice for. Then to the Quinko ruins. They weren't that exciting. Back to Cuzco where we checked into a hotel. Finally, the 3 S's. Big restaurant feast tonight. Peruvian soup, filet mignon, dessert along with Peruvian music. We all went dancing after dinner.

The next day started off by renting equipment for the Inca Trail hike. The afternoon I spent walking around Cuzco, taking in the churches and doing some shopping. Evening was spent packing for the hike.

On the eighteenth day, we started with an early 4:30 wake up. We had to catch a six in the morning local train to KM88 to start the hike on the Inca trail. A massive crowd jammed into the train station. A squished person I was. What a sight. People jamming into the train. Peruvians going up and down the crowded aisles selling bread, coffee, cakes, all kinds of stuff. Even a half blind singer blaring away. Crates of chickens shoved under seats. The ride was very uncomfortable but very interesting. Finally KM88. This is the starting point of the Inca Trail to reach Machu Pichu-The Lost City. The trail was discarded in 1915. Several years later, it was made fit for tourists as the trail crosses mountains and valleys with alternating climbs and descents.

We had to dart off the train as the conductor doesn't like waiting. The big challenge right away was crossing the Urhambra River to start the hike. We took the "Flying Fox"-an open platform for three people to ride across pushed along by a local. Rushing river below. The first part of the climb is the hardest as it includes the first range going over 4000 M. The trail is paved with Inca relics and archaeological sites. The best were called Sayacmarca and Huinya Huayna. Late afternoon we set up camp in a field. A steer was walking around, bumping into the tents.

An 8AM start after a breakfast of soup and coffee. Another long day of climbing up and down. I met other hikers along the way. A camaraderie develops even though we have language barriers. It felt good to crawl back in the tent for the night after a semi dinner but good conversation with the other adventurers.

Again, the next day was another day of hiking. Going down hill. Steep down hill. It had rained during the night. We ended up slipping down the trail. The weather was great for hiking. Made it to Camp 1. Approaching Machu Picchu from this direction is an extraordinary experience.

Rounding the bend of Puerto Del Sol (The Gate of the Sun) the entire Lost City suddenly appears.

It was now New Year's Eve Day. Rain and fog when we woke. We waited until nine for the fog to lift to see another of the Wonders of the World-Machu Picchu. It took 1/2 hour to climb down to the Lost City. It was amazing to think how this city was built. How these stones were brought up the mountain to build a city. The stone boulders connected like a puzzle. To this day, no one knows exactly why Machu Picchu was abandoned. Walking around, I saw row upon row of carefully crafted terraces. Open rooms upon rooms you enter and wonder. One of the sites, the Temple of the Three Windows is made entirely of one block of stone, in which three large windows have been carved with precision. Machu Picchu was a well-planned city with its temples, fortresses and remarkable construction.

We took the tourist train back to Cuzco. A more relaxing trip then the local train up. Being New Year's Eve, we went to Vic's American Café. I actually found peanut butter there. I walked around the plaza. We went to bed at 2am after a night of reminiscing about the hike.

New Year's Day. January 1. Left Cuzco about 11. Visited Picca Picawa and Tambo Machay ruins. Ate lunch at Allytaytambo and looked around the town. Major problem. We were supposed to go around the country, starting in Lima and ending in Lima. With only a fourth of the journey left, we could not continue onward. Terrorist problems in the city of Ayachucho. Bridges to this city have been blown up. The Shining Path Maoist Underground was acting up. Lots of killings. We were advised to go back. So it was back to Nazca, then to Lima. Constant road travel. Hole in radiator in Nazca. A temporary stop to get the truck fixed. We finally made it back to Lima. A married couple from England asked if they would get a partial refund since we had to retrace our route for two days to get back. Would they rather have gone through Ayachucho? I think not. Remember, any time you are on an adventure trip, you have to be flexible as anything can alter your plans.

Back in Lima, we visited the rich suburb of Mira Floris to see how the affluent lived. A whole different world with nice homes and shops. It's been a week since we left Cuzco. Thirty days out. I packed into some sleazy hotel room with six others. Thin walls. The Peruvian couple next door were going at it at two in the morning. She was a real moaner. I yelled "come already, so we can get some sleep!" Up at 5:30. Had to catch the plane home. I was ready to go home.

The difference in losing luggage on a trip in the states and losing luggage on an adventure trip in another part of the world, can be like night and day. It's easy to get tracked down in the state and hope that your luggage catches up with you. If not, it is not too difficult to get the needed necessities. Now consider you're in a third world country without your luggage. You're traveling in such a way that a piece of luggage may not catch up with you. It is also difficult to start shopping in foreign surroundings. You have no idea where to go and don't have the language skills to ask and get around quickly. Luckily, I had the day to get my lost luggage. Next time, I will bring enough on the plane to get by if this should happen again. Another idea is to leave a day early just in case a flight is missed or delayed. Maybe, you'll need a day to recover your lost luggage. If you have to be someplace, getting there a day early will not turn into a panic situation should something go wrong. If all runs smoothly, you have a free day to enjoy.

CHAPTER 5

▼

THAILAND: USING A TICKET BROKER

Our journey in Northern Thailand explores the Golden Triangle Opium Trail, cruises by rice barge down twisting jungle rivers, and includes a 5-day foot trek to isolated hill tribes villages around Changmai.

It had been three years since my last major trip. The problem was that I was low on funds. I had taken the last two summers off by playing camp counselor in upstate New York and a third summer outside of Boston. These had been great summers as I taught canoeing, basic wilderness survival and even became a camp program director. I made some good friends and was a kid again. However, this was no way for a thirty-something man to make a living. Trying to sell real estate and not being around is not very financially rewarding.

Then it came. An end to my life. I went to work for a major corporation. I had been a working stiff. Now I was a working dead stiff. No more three months off in the summer running canoe programs. No more month long trips to foreign lands. Could I survive?

It turned out to be for the best. My job demanded a lot of traveling. By air. With my receiving frequent flyer miles. Republic Airlines which merged into Northwest Airlines became my partner.

Now I had to find a place to travel. I got catalogs from different adventure travel operators. I had to make use of holiday weekends to get the most days I could with the fourteen I had for vacation. I chose to travel with an outfit called Explore to Thailand on their Golden Triangle trip. Again, I chose an inexpensive trip as no cook would be along and accommodations would not be The Ritz.

Air travel for business I thought would be glamorous, jet set, and such. I found out real fast how boring business travel is. After spending twenty-six hours on the plane to get from Minneapolis to Bangkok, I didn't want to fly again. You also learn about delays, missed connections and such. My flight to Thailand had me leaving Minneapolis to Seattle. Then Seattle to Kyoto, Kyoto to Bangkok. I used a ticket broker. I had some frequent flyer tickets that I sold. I made enough money selling my frequent flyer miles from Northwest Airlines to purchase a business class ticket on United Airlines. I had called ads from the paper selling fly-rights. The ones I sold would not get me to Thailand. I didn't know what to expect or how trustworthy the people on the other line were. I compared prices and the best deal was from a travel agency in California. Buying and selling frequent flyer tickets was a side business. I used a credit card to purchase the tickets. The tickets came. Everything worked out great. All on the up and up.

I met the group in Bangkok. A chap named Charlie from England was to be my roommate. Nice guy. However, he was still living at home at age 34. We all got a quick lesson on what would happen if caught with or dealing drugs. A sign in the restaurant said that Westerners came to Thailand thinking drugs are allowed and free flowing.

If you should be caught using, dealing, smuggling drugs the following would happen:

Heroin:
>   Processing, Smuggling for Sale: Execution
>   Processing, Smuggling: Life
>   Selling, Possession For Sale: 5 years to Life
>   Possession: 1 to 10 years

Morphine:
>   Processing, Smuggling for Sale: 20 years
>   Processing, Smuggling: 1 to 10 years
>   Possession: up to 5 years
>   Possession For Sale: 1 to 10 years
>   Use: up to 10 years

Marijuana:
>   Processing, Sale, Smuggling: 2 to 15 years
>   Possession For Sale: 2 to 15 years
>   Possession: up to 5 years
>   Use: up to 1 year

Opium:
>   Selling, Smuggling: 1 to 20 years
>   Possession: 1 to 10 years
>   Use: 1 to 10 years

That was a quick education. Especially during the trip when we learned of two Australians being hung in Malaysia for trafficking in drugs.

The first couple of days were spent getting organized and playing tourist in the big city. An early morning trip by boat along the busy canals (K Longs) to see the floating market of Old Thon Buri. Along the way, we see school age children on docks waiting for a boat bus to pick them up for school. The floating markets are a very important part of local life. We see colorfully dressed Thai's selling a wide variety of vegetables, exotic fruits and flowers from small boats. From here we saw the temples. Temple of Dawn, Marble Temple and the popular Reclining and Golden Buddha. For lunch we were at an ordinary cafeteria. Too touristy. Four of us went to find our own lunch including crazy George, a truck driver from Malta living in Australia. We would become good friends. As we wandered the streets, we saw many small eating areas. All had rice with some kind of glop put over it. So when in Thailand, do as the Thai's do. We sat down, had a plate of rice with that day's glop on it. I took a mouthful. The pain of mouth on fire came instantly. I have never tasted spicy food like this. I tried calling out for water but I couldn't speak. The locals around started laughing, tears were in my eyes. I was very careful about what glop was on my rice from then on.

At night, we wandered the streets. We sneaked a peak at a sex show. It was a porno movie come to life. Right on stage. We didn't go in. It could have become very costly in more ways than one. Dinner that night was rice-with glop. However, the glop had been "Westernized" and easy to eat.

The next day, we hopped on an air-conditioned bus for a 9-hour ride to Chaing Mai. Beautiful countryside as we passed through many small towns and saw plenty of rice paddies. That night we were able to stay in a fairly nice hotel. During the couple of days we would spend in Chaing Mai, we would play tourist. Visiting the hilltop monastery of Do Suthep at 3,500 feet was a spectacular site. We even had a shot at the fortune sticks. This monastery is famed for its Buddha relics and attracts pilgrimages from all over the country. Also visited the traditional cottage industries-cotton weaving, wood carving, silk with bowls of silk worms, silver and laquer ware. I got a small vase made out of pieces of egg shells. Walked around the town at night. We never felt that we were in any danger. The people were very friendly.

The next day we viewed an elephant training center. Elephants are work horses for the people. Elephants are trained commands by the Mahout. Elephants can be trained only because they agree to be trained. They could, with one swipe of their trunks, kill a Mahout. Elephants work 4-5 hours a day and when they feel like quitting, they quit. If it is too hot, they don't work. I like their work ethic. I wish I could work 4 hours a day and quit when I felt like it.

Then we climbed aboard for an elephant ride in the jungle. A little baby elephant stayed close behind as it followed it's mother. What a sight. About eight elephants lumbering through the jungle. From the hot elephants we jumped in a river for a swim, then climbed aboard a wooden raft for some light river rafting. Found a pool of water for more swimming, and a waterfall to huddle under for a group photo. That evening we had a briefing of the next four days which were to be our trek to isolated hill tribe villages. We will have hills to climb, rivers to cross and bugs to drink our blood.

We travel by truck north to Mae Suai village. Then start the trek to a small Akha tribal village high in the surrounding hills. There are no roads here, but you can hear them coming. We arrive at a village and set up in the headman's hut. Our sleeping floor is bamboo. We're all together in one big room.

The children gather around. They are curious. I have a set of jacks and start playing with a couple of kids. Cheap thrills but everyone is enjoying themselves. Dinner that night is, you guessed it, rice with glop. Watching the way of life is very interesting to me. Basically, the people are farmers. However, their customs are very different based on centuries of tradition. Most of the remaining six distinctive tribes live in the northern hills at an altitude between 3,000 and 4,000 feet. The people drifted down from China, Laos, and Burma. They lead simple lives away from the social tensions and complexities of urban living.

The next day was a trek through high grasses, open land and river crossing. The weather was beautiful. We spent the next night with the Lahu. I had balloons which I filled with water and tossed water balloons around with the kids. This was big time. Kids loved it. I enjoyed mingling with them. There was no verbal communication. Just a lot of smiles and laughter. I wish we were able to communicate. We did some communicating with the help of our guide. We met the chief. He is 31 years old. He is chief because he is the best. However, he doesn't like being chief. He has to travel to Chaing Mai once a month. Gives a report on what's happening.

Who was born, who died, crop report and so on. A missionary lived here. He had married a Lahu woman. I asked him about the impending roads. He said it was good and bad. Bad that modern civilization may inhabit their simple way of life, but good as they can get needed medicine. The Lahu did not cultivate opium as the Akha tribe had done for us the previous night. While the men worked the field in the Lahu tribe, the Akha women work the fields. This is because the men are stoned from opium. Children over age 11 join their mothers in the field. The men stay in the village. The men smoke, sleep, eat, then smoke, sleep, eat again. If the police come, they hide it. However, the police come on foot so the men have ample warning. School is for kids 7 to 10 years old. School is taught by a teacher from Chaing Mai. A teacher may only come once a month. Kids are taught the Thai language and metric system. Girls marry at age 15, men at 20. The young men join their fathers in a stupor. They know it's bad for them but follow in their father's way. We were invited in to their den of sin. Naturally, we did not want to offend our hosts and indulged.

Stayed with a Lisu tribe the third night. They dressed up in their colorful clothing and did a traditional dance for us. Both men and women work in the field. They grow rice and corn. They also hunt for their food. Catch squirrel, rabbit, wild boar. Our meal each night was rice with probably meat from one of these animals. I didn't want to know.

We make our way back to Mae Suai to arrange for a truck to pick us up to drive us to Chaing Mai. Able to get a hotel room where a normal shower felt good. We gathered for dinner to plan an evening. Crazy George and Derrick, the two Australians, wanted to visit a brothel. This perked up the ears of my roommate, Charles. Quiet and soft spoken, he was coming alive. A couple others jumped on the bandwagon. I took Charley under my wing and explained why it would not be a good idea to have intercourse. Go for the oral. Our guide, Chan Intawong, explained that the girls were tested and free from disease. Yeah, right, I thought.

Never know who they were with an hour before. I went along. Just to see the place and to keep an eye on Charley.

She was beautiful. What can I say. We commandeered a couple of bike taxis. Entering, we walked a long hallway to a room where we saw girls sitting behind a lighted glass wall with numbers. The cost of 8 baht was for a massage. Hell, I couldn't be a party pooper. She was so beautiful, number 87. I paid my 8 baht and was led into a room. When it was over, 20 baht later, 87 and I sat out in the lobby. I asked Chan to tell her I wanted to bring her back home with me. Finally, we were all together in the lobby. We said our good-byes and headed back to the hotel. Charley had a big smile on his face. I had a big worry. It was going to worry me for the next six years. I didn't practice what I preached.

The next day we headed north from Chaing Mai by pick-up truck to the Burmese frontier post at Mai Sai. In the afternoon, we arrived at the famous Golden Triangle, the confluence of rivers which form the point where Burma, Laos and Thailand meet. The region is notorious for the opium trade, controlled by a number of private armies. We stay at a simple bungalow on the bank of the Mekong River, right in the Golden Triangle. The night was kind of eerie. My imagination ran wild with banditos breaking down the doors, shooting us as we lay in bed.

I woke up alive. We walked the bridgeway into Burma. However, we can't enter as we don't have visas, nor were we planning on it.

We head back to Chaing Mai. We reclaim our main luggage that we didn't need for the trek. A couple of us had dinner at a street cafe. Rice and glop. We sat for a couple of hours and talked. No way do they hustle you out of the restaurant as they do in the states.

We leave Chaing Mai by bus for a 5-hour drive to Nakhon Sawar. We will embark on a converted rice barge downstream on the winding Chao Phya River. We will be spending two nights on this rig. Nothing to do on the boat except read, write, talk, sleep and look at the scenery as we travel slowly down river. We visit the temple at Sing Buri and get the feel of the authentic life of the river dwellers and boat people.

The bathroom is unique. A little outhouse shaped area on back corner of barge. Open door. Grab inside bar. Position feet on boards. Two boards on each side with the river in between. Hold onto bar as you turn around facing door. Drop pants, squat. Aim between the two boards you are standing on to have your doings drop into the river. Gross by all standards.

We arrive at the old capital of Siam, destroyed by the Burmese in 1767. After seeing the monuments of Ayudhya, we go by minibus the final 50 miles to Bangkok.

Final group dinner. Group picture. Exchange of addresses. Roam the streets for last minute souvenirs. Breakfast the next morning and then the hard part. Saying good-bye to your close knit family of 18 days. Hugs and tears. Knowing we shared an incredible adventure together but it's time for farewell. We would not meet again. Or would we?

CHAPTER 6

▼

DARIEN GAP:
JUNGLE TREK OF A LIFETIME

A traverse of the barely penetrable Darien Gap by canoe and on foot is surely one of the most incredible jungle treks in the world.

The Darien lies as an almost total physical barrier across the Central American isthmus cutting off communities to the north and south. This magnificent region of absolutely untouched tropical forest situated between two great oceans has a somewhat exaggerated, if not undeserved, reputation as "hostile to man."

The Darien is the largest province in Panama, the least developed and most sparsely populated.

I had been dreaming about this trip for seven years. When I first started reading the adventure travel catalogs, this trip always stood out to me. It seemed the most challenging and most remote area closest to home. The Pan American Highway which runs from the tip of North America to the bottom of South America is a continuous highway except for the area of the Darien. The land is too rugged. Jungle too thick. This was going to be my ultimate challenge. I think I've said that before. However, I knew this trip would be a challenge. Extreme heat and humidity and the need to carry optimum loads, placed very precise emphasis on equipment needs. We would be out trekking for nine days. Full pack loads as we would be carrying food for all the days.

My first chore would be getting the time off. Sixteen days. The trip would start in Panama City and end in Cartagena, Columbia. What adventure travel outfit would I go with? There were only two I was looking at. One outfit had the dates I wanted with a cost of $2,000. Encounter Overland would cost $1,100, but didn't have the dates I preferred. Calling the first outfit to inquire why their trip was priced at $2,000 while their competitor was $1,100, I learned they stayed in better accommodations. I asked if this meant air-conditioned tents. Really, what kind of better accommodations can you get camping in the jungle. You have a tarp, netting and a sheet. They also said the guides are top notch and a privilege to travel with. Designer jeans came to mind. I opted for Encounter Overland. I worked the days out with my boss. I would be gone over Christmas and New Year's. This would give me an extra four free vacation days. I needed this as I only had two weeks of vacation.

After I got all this taken care of, the hard part came. Getting in shape. I wasn't overweight. I was just in blah shape. I had to build up endurance. The jogging started. It was winter, so I did laps at the Y. Filled my back pack up to climb up and down my basement stairs. Watched what I ate. It's hard to do all this while working a stressful, demanding corporate work day.

A visa was needed for Columbia. Vaccinations needed updating. Malaria pills acquired. I would be going from the dead of a Minnesota winter to the oven of the Darien Gap.

It was time to go. No problems in departing. I arrived in Panama City a day before I needed to meet the group. Not knowing anything or anywhere,

I headed to the Holiday Inn. Some adventurer I was. It was hot and I knew it would be hotter.

I walked around the area. I found out what hotel I was to meet the group at. I did nothing spectacular and ate in the confines of the Holiday Inn. I practiced my Espanol. Nice and comfy in my hotel room. Who knows what is in store for me tomorrow. Once again, I start wondering why I'm here? Why am I doing this? The trip sounded fantastic when I first read about it years previous. I only imagined doing this. Again, as the time came when I could take this trip, I started telling my friends about it. As usual, no great interest from them. They couldn't imagine why anyone would do such a trip. The loneliness of an adventure traveler. Here I was, all by myself in a foreign land. Just yesterday I was at work. Now I was going to embark on my most physically demanding trip yet. The jungles of the Darien. I was going to dare the Darien.

I met the group at El Colon Hotel. This hotel was just above sleaze. In fact, we were told not to walk south, even one block, as that was an area notorious for trouble. There were nine guys and one girl. From London to Switzerland. The best thing about these trips is the international flavor of the participants. Our guide was a novice. He had just trained by going through the Darien by way of Cartagena to Panama. Now he was going to lead us from Panama to Cartagena. We learned about the load we would be packing, the route and the need to trek long hours to reach rivers to camp by. Money would not be a problem. There was no place to spend it. We put everything not needed that was brought along in a suitcase to be shipped to Cartagena. This was mostly everything because we would be carrying food, cookware, camping gear needed for the next seven days. How I longed for the comfort of the Holiday Inn.

The Darien is an intact wilderness, largely protect by it's inaccessibility. This is where the Pan American Highway ends so our transportation will be mostly by foot and dugout canoe. We will drive to Yaviza. Then we will take a boat and trail route which runs through the forest to the Columbia boarder via the villages of Boca De Cupe, Pucuro, and Paya. The area is not well marked. No hotels or restaurants. It is a route for drug smugglers and illegal aliens. Also, Columbia guerrillas operate in the region. However, the chaotic and dictatorial rule made Panama City not so fun to be in.

It was time to go. Gathering all our gear we boarded an old bus to head east along the Panama Isthmus. Fairly good road to Chepobut. Gravel and mud tracks to Yaviza. This was going to be an all day affair. I was tired from the long travel day and anxious on what lies ahead. The next day we were going into the Darien as the road ended here in Yaviza. For the next two days we travel up the Tuira River and its upper streams by motorized canoe. At night we stayed in Cuna and Choco Indian villages. The Choco communities are spectacular, primitive, cooled by the river and with a peace that only a village with no roads can manage. It was Christmas week. Their Christmas tree was a leafless tree with old tin cans hanging from the bare branches. The school house was simple where just the basics of the language was taught along with a monetary system. They must have had some kind of satellite feed or old tape as that night a movie was playing. Advertised as action, action, people gathered around an old TV set.

The people were very friendly. They went on with their daily lives. Me Espanol no muy bueno. Therefore, it was hard to communicate. With their Indian dialect, I had no hope anyway. The children were curious, as usual. Our room that night was an open air hut.

We continued to the village of Boca de Cupe by canoe. The streams are smaller and at times we have to push the canoes through shallow stretches. Then it is on foot. Jungle trails and river crossings. I slipped and fell on the first river crossing. Water waist high and a very slippery bottom. The weather was 90 degree heat and 90 percent humidity. The vegetation was so thick that at times we got lost. This was jungle by the truest sense of the word. We hiked 50 minutes with 10 minute rests. I was a slow hiker but the girl was even slower, so I had a companion. At times, we would lead which slowed the pace. Even though we would only cover about 10-12 miles per day, the thick mud and waist deep river crossing together with the heat and humidity along with the difficulty of the path meant six to eight hour walking days. Drinking water was a problem as large quantities were required to avoid dehydration. Canteens were empty in no time. Coming across another serpentine river crossing, we filled our canteens and drank. Drank before even purifying the water. We were in an exhaustive, thirsty condition.

It was getting dark and we had to cut away a clearing to set up camp. We set up a tarp between two trees and claimed a ground spot to crash. Out in the open air along with all the creatures and bugs of the jungle night. I took off my sweat filled clothes for the night only to put on cold, still wet by sweat clothes on the next morning. I lay there that night thinking I must be insane. Why, why, why? The answer was always the same. Whether I was here dying in the heat of the Darien, or on some other adventure, this is where I was supposed to be. Speaking of dying, I did just that. During the 10 minute breaks, I couldn't cool down. I would drink, but that just sweated off. My pace was slow. I was struggling. I had always been the one to help others. Now I needed help. I couldn't go on. I just wanted to roll over on the leaf ants path and have the ants carry me off. Take me now. Cart me away. I can't go on. I was white as a ghost. Heat exhaustion caught up to me. Coming from the tundra of Minnesota to the inferno of the Darien was too much for this old body. I did not acclimatize as the others had. Here we were in the heart of the jungle. No ambulance to get me. No gas station up ahead to call AAA. It was another couple of days before we would reach the ranger outpost of Kathos National Park. Talk about transporting me out by helicopter once we reached the outpost was mentioned. We had to move on now. The rest of the group divided up my pack. I was able to walk and cool down.

We crossed the border of Panama and Columbia at Palo de Las Letras. The only thing to mark this area was a plaque which we all stood around and took a picture. From here we traveled to Los Katios National Park in Cristales. I was feeling stronger. I just felt bad because the others had to carry my gear. The packs did get lighter as food was eaten which lightened the load. Upon arriving at the National Park, I just fell flat. Relieved that the long hiking days were over. Over were the days of putting on wet, cold clothes. I just collapsed from exhaustion. I then filled my canteen and drank. Refilled it and drank. Sat naked in the river and finally cooled down and drank some more. I put on fresh, dry clothes. I was anew, a calming refreshed feeling. I was in heaven. I slept good that night. The next day I did some short day hikes in the park to view waterfalls, cascades, monkeys and iguanas.

We were back to motorized canoe crossing the Atrato swamps. We came across a woman washing clothes in the river. Her two young boys played above the hill and stared down on us. It looked like they were eating the leaves off the bushes. One of the kids came and sat by me. He was about six years old. I thought I'd try my Spanish on him. I asked him to "venir a me casa en America." To my sorprendor, my surprise, he smiled and shook his head. Shit, now what do I do? I think I asked him if he would like to come to my house in America. I wondered if I was even understood.

The woman showed us her home. A simple open home with roof and walls. A hard ground floor for sleeping, an open area for cooking. Very basic. Very poor. The kids, though, were as happy as could be. No TV's, no video games. Just playing around in nature. They were rich in my eyes. We said good-bye and thank you as we were leaving. I looked back at the six-year old. He had a look as if he was saying, "how about me?"

We continued on, set up camp and got to bed early as we would have to wake up at five in the morning. We needed to do this to catch a calm saltwater Bahia Columbia Sea to Turbo. Getting up in pure outdoor jungle darkness was eerie. The sea was calm. We crossed the river in pre-dawn light. It turned out to be an easy crossing to Turbo. What a dump, the town of Turbo. Like an old shipyard. We stayed here just long enough to catch a bus. It would be five hours to Arboletes. On the way we were stopped by the Columbia military. They had us stand by the bus and collected our passports. I heard the word "gringo" and was just waiting to be pulled aside, tortured and shot. Left for dead. After a short while we were on our way for the nine hour ride to Cartagena.

It was New Year's Eve Day. Christmas had come and gone in the jungles of the Darien. Tonight, we would party in Cartagena. Arriving in Cartagena, we went to a motel. A motel. Finally, a place for the three S's. Shit, shower, shave. There were four single beds to our room. Judy, the only girl, was in my room. I took off my clothes and was heading toward the bathroom when Judy said, "My God! Look at you!"

I said "I'm sorry if I don't have the most attractive butt."

She said "Look."

I had bite marks all over the back of my body. Insect bite marks. I must have had company in my camp bed last night. However, this wasn't going to stop me of my enjoyment on the other side of the door. Upon getting in the bathroom, a frown came across my face. To be delicate, I'll say this. Toilet paper cannot be flushed. It had to be tossed in the basket next to the toilet. The nozzle for the shower head was a sock. Talk about being bummed out. A major bummer. The water trickled down the sock. No water pressure. Shaving was difficult along with the other hygiene items I was trying to take care of.

I roamed the streets of Cartagena. The fascinating aspects of the city are the fortress-like walls that surround the city. The fort was originally built as protection against pirates. San Felipe Fortress is considered the masterpiece of Spanish engineering built between 1536 and 1657. This massive fort commands a magnificent view of the approaches to Cartagena. The fort sits 135 feet above sea level. We explored the fortresses network of subterranean tunnels and galleries. We looked over the cannons protecting the fort.

That evening was New Year's Eve. Nothing too much exciting going on. Some dancing in the streets and then to bed right after midnight.

The next day, I just laid on the beach. I talked to an American businessman who was down here for an immersion into the language. This is the only way to really learn. That evening we had our farewell dinner. We reflected on what we had accomplished. I could only say thanks for assist-ing me through the trip when I felt I couldn't go on.

I was to catch a six in the evening flight. I again laid on the beach until around two. I got cleaned up. I finished packing and said my last good-byes. As usual, good-byes are never easy.

I arrived at the airport well before departure. I just wanted to get through Customs and Immigration without any delays. I was out of pesos. I was set to leave. Since I was there early, I was first to check in. Immigration did not start for a couple hours so I hung around Rafael Nunez Airport. I had checked my internal frame backpack so a small carry-on was all I had with me. I made myself comfortable in a chair across from the door to which I would go through Immigration. It was time to reflect on my past adventure. A time to realize another adventure complete. A line started to form by the Immigration door. I got out of the chair and took a place in line. A glass wall separated the general area to the departure area which was past Immigration. They stamped my passport and I took a seat in the departure area. When it was time, the doors would open and we would be led out on the tarmac to the plane. Armed policia were guarding the door, the departure area started filling up. Then from back at the Immigration desk, shouting. People banging on the glass wall. Screaming Spanish. The policia guarding the doors broke into a run to the Immigration desk. I couldn't see what was going on. Nor did I care. I was here just waiting to get on the plane. Some official came down to the area to speak to the crowd. I had no idea what she was saying. The Spanish was too fast. Shouting started from some people. They got up and started pushing towards the doors that led out to the tarmac. I joined in. I found an English-speaking person. "What was going on?" It seems the plane we were all to get on was full. Only a few seats were available. Even if you had a ticket, it would do you no good today. The plane we were to take to Miami had originated in Medellin and more passengers than expected got on there. The people pushed open the doors. The policia came running back. They were trying to hold people back, allowing one at a time through. People with babies and strollers were not going to make it. Older people were not going to make it. Businessmen with carry-on luggage were not going to make it. This gringo was going to make it. I joined in the pushing then ducked under everybody. My short stature finally rewarded me. I broke through the crowd. The official yelled at me for my ticket. I held it up to show I was legitimate. She waved me by, as someone else had to be dealt with. I ran in the darkness looking for the plane. I saw some official and asked, "Donde es el airoplano a Miami?" She pointed "aqui." I ran up the steps. Plane looked full. I got in the cabin and looked for an open seat. Even in desperation, I first checked for an aisle seat. No luck. Grabbed a middle seat between two women. Sweating, I took a cloth from my bag to wipe my face. I took a magazine from the seat pouch. Even though it was in Spanish, I pretended to read. I wanted to blend in. The reason. There were people in the plane unable to find a seat and were being escorted off. We finally took off and the bingo games started.

CHAPTER 7

▼

COSTA RICA: SHORT ADVENTURES

Quick adventure to Costa Rica. I had a week in February to get away from winter. I wanted to go river rafting and see a different country. Through a different adventure travel outfitter, I found what I was looking for. Or at least, what I thought I was looking for.

We met at a hotel in San Jose, capital city of Costa Rica. A small group of eight including the trip leader. What amazed me about San Jose and I think the country in general, the police do not carry guns. This was back in 1987. Street crime has increased in the 1990's and gangs called "chapulines" operate in upscale areas as well as slums. Health-wise, Costa Rica has among the highest standards of public health in Latin America and works aggressively to minimize disease. In 1970, Costa Rica created a national park system which has become one of the best in the world.

The first days of the trip were the best. River rafting on the Class IV Pacuare River. The Pacuare was declared Costa Rica's first wild and scenic river just the previous year. The trip which lasted three days was a thrill. Exciting whitewater and beautiful country. The Pacuare passes through a deep, heavily forested gorge where local Indians still hunt and where you can see increasingly rare wildlife. At night we would camp out along the banks of the Pacuare. The scenery was beautiful. I was enjoying the rafting immensely.

After the rafting, we took an old DC-3 to the other side-Gulf side of Costa Rica. Here our guide led us on a nature walk and we laid on the beach for sun and swim. This was boring. No adventure here. I palled up with Christopher from Ohio and Clark from California. We were getting bummed out. Nothing exciting planned for the next few days. So we decided to make our own adventure. We told our guide we would meet them the last night for the farewell dinner. But for now it was farewell. We were going back to San Jose and do our own thing. I think we stunned the poor guy. We told him it was nothing against him, we just wanted more. We did just that. We took the plane back to San Jose, rented a car and did our own sight-seeing, including the cloud forest of Monteverde. It can be a clear day, yet there is a cloud hanging over this national park. Strange sight to see. Monteverde is a wonderful park to stroll through. During the years since I was there, trams and canopy walkways were developed, giving visitors the ability to see the tops of the forest canopy.

While driving the freeway, a motorcycle cop pulled me over. He said I was speeding. Now here was the problem. He only spoke Spanish. He knew no English. The Spanish I knew did no good, nor did I pretend to know what he was saying. What he was saying was I was to pay a fine to him or else go to the police station. I kept saying no comprendo. I don't understand. The policeman was getting pissed. I kept insinuating, I don't understand. Finally, he threw up his arms, muttered to himself and left. Clark, Chris and I had a good laugh.

That was about it. We met the group for a farewell dinner and left the next day. Chris came with me to Fort Lauderdale where my parents lived and we spent a couple of days there.

This was a simple trip I could have planned myself. There are a lot of whitewater river outfitters. We went with Costa Rica Expeditions who did a fine job. I just didn't have the time to plan it. However, it wouldn't have been very hard or time consuming. I was getting to the point where I thought, it's time to plan and do my own trips.

This is the question you have to ask yourself. Is it worth your time to go with an organized adventure group? Can you go along with a planned itinerary? Will you feel you have no freedom to do what you want? How much time and energy do you have to plan a trip? Whether you go with an adventure group, a trip sponsored by your place of worship, AAA, airlines, whatever. I have always had good luck and enjoyed traveling with adventure tour operators. However, on this trip to Costa Rica, I wanted more.

CHAPTER 8

▼

BORNEO: ANTICIPATIONS
AND CHALLENGES

The primeval and impenetrable jungles of Borneo were once the home of fierce head hunters, known as the Sea Dyak. Legends about the island's inaccessibility were put about by early seafarers and travelers. Today, Borneo remains a true adventurer's destination.

Two years had passed since my last adventure. I was now over 40 years old. What kind of trip could I go on? How much could I do? I was in relatively good shape, but sitting all day playing corporate man did make the body kind of lazy. I belonged to a health club. I jog when I get to it. Now I will have to get to it.

The adventure begins when I gather my adventure catalogs. Even though I said my next trip would be planned by me, I lied. I didn't make the time to plan an extensive adventure. Plus, I would book through Adventure Center and know I would get adventure. So, as usual, where to go? My choices were quickly narrowed. The trip could be no more than two weeks in length. The destination had to be a place reached by Northwest Airlines. I had frequent flyer miles. That left me with Central America, Europe or Southeast Asia. The trip was going to be in December, so that left out Europe. I couldn't find any trip that would work in Central America. That left Southeast Asia. I had been to Thailand. Thailand had been my last adventure trip. Then I saw it. There it was in all its glory. Borneo Adventure. Fourteen days and I could fly into Bangkok, catch a flight to Kuala Lumpur, Malaysia and fly out of Singapore. So be it. Borneo.

I have a childhood friend. We have been best buds since sixth grade. Still together. We're still close. I had enough frequent flyer mileage for two people to take the trip. Barry always envied my taking off on adventures. Sitting in my car one day, I read him the description of the Borneo Adventure. I said this is where I'm thinking of going next. He listened and said he wished he could go. "Then you shall," I said and plopped the airline tickets on his lap. He was stunned. I said, "the most expensive part of the trip is getting there. Getting there is my treat. The land cost would be your expense. This amounted to about $1,100,"

"My wife will divorce me," Barry said.

"What better reason for you to go," I replied. Poor Barry. Didn't know what to do. This would have been a dream. Barry owned a drugstore. He was a hardworking pharmacist. A real working stiff. He would think about it. See what he could do.

About two weeks later, Barry told me he couldn't go. He said his Dad was sick, he had a store to run.

"Barry," I said, "Let me reach in my pocket. Look what I found. A hand full of excuses, you're too tall, too short, too fat, too thin-which excuse do you want? I got a whole pocket full." Barry just dropped his head. Hell, I can hear his wife bitching on what a crazy idea this was.

So it went. Barry couldn't go. No problem for me. I used the mileage I would have given to him, and used it on myself to upgrade to business class.

I started whipping myself into shape. Jogging, stationary bike, stair climbing. I didn't want to die like I did in the Darien Jungle. I got the Visas. I got my vaccinations updated. I bought a carry bag that doubled as a backpack. I was getting in shape and losing weight. I loved the preparation.

It was getting close to departure. No one to talk to about it. No one to get excited about the trip with. I felt I was in shape and ready to go. I received the trip dossier. I was to get to the Malaysia Hotel in Kuala Lumpur. Good luck to me.

As I start my next adventure, I always wonder what really lies ahead. How will I be tested? What challenges will I cope with? The trip included a climb up Mount Kinabulu to 13,255 feet. Would I be up to the challenge?

The first challenge started before I left. The night before departure, it was snowing. The first big storm of winter would greet the morning rush-hour traffic. The roads could be snowy, icy. I called my sister, Bonnie and her husband, John, to pick me up at seven-thirty the next morning, 15 minutes earlier than our previous arrangement. Waking up hearing the morning weather report, I heard that the storm did not hit. Getting to the airport was easy. So things started off fine-for a second. As I got to the airline counter to check in for my flight which was to Seattle then to Tokyo-switch planes in Tokyo to Bangkok-I encountered a problem. Delay-no plane. Instead of a nine-twenty flight, a new plane would be leaving at twelve noon. Being a frequent flyer, I knew what I would encounter. A further delay. Then an even further delay. Then cancellation. I had to get to Bangkok to get my flight on Thai Airlines to Kuala Lumpur.

I asked at the counter what options I had. The Northwest Airlines counter person produced a miracle. She said wait and left for fifteen minutes. She came back with a boarding pass to San Francisco which was leaving in a half-hour. I would change planes in San Francisco to flight 351 leaving for Bangkok, Thailand to arrive on time.

During the four-hour plane ride to San Francisco, I listened to the comedy of Bill Cosby over the plane radio and wonder if anyone sees my chuckling. I watch the movie "The Dead Poet's Society."

Things are going smoothly. The plane leaving San Francisco is on time. I even got a seat on the upper deck. It's like a little club car. I found out this plane makes a stop in Tokyo before going on to Bangkok. The trip to Tokyo is eleven hours and from Tokyo to Bangkok, another six hours. The big question is when to sleep to avoid jet lag. It probably wouldn't matter anyhow. Right now its noon Pacific time and I think three in the morning, Bangkok time. So I should go to sleep right now to start adjusting. Lucky me, no one is sitting next to me. I can stretch out.

I received an overseas airline goody bag. Shaving cream and razor. Powdered mouthwash, just add water. Emery board, toothbrush, toothpaste. Moisturizing cream, comb, socks and a mask. I'll try and sleep. Take my contacts out and give sleep a try.

Partially failed. Dozed for four hours. Missed the meal but didn't care. Now I've got to try and stay awake until Bangkok. Read, listen to music, glance at the movie, which was-what else-Dead Poet's Society. Getting hungry now but nothing I can get. Almost 1 1/2 hours before Tokyo and a light snack is being served. Last meal I had was a cheese omelet going to San Francisco some fourteen hours ago. Now I get Espanole Quiche with fruit garnish.

Even though this flight #27 is continuing on to Bangkok, we must get off. I don't know what time it is here. It's two in the morning back home. I'm starting to turn into a zombie. I need sleep but can't. I find out it's 3PM Bangkok time. I need to adjust to this time period. I have to wait in the transient lounge about an hour before boarding again. I gotta stay awake.

The happy travelers boarded the plane. You know who they are. The husband and wife team who are on their once-in-a-lifetime trip and let people know they are there. The wife is loud and oh, so sweet. I think I'll throw up. I'm getting punchy from lack of sleep. The menu-steak or fish.

I'm ready for breakfast food. Now the stewardess gives me another travel bag. I guess you can never have enough sleeping masks.

Arrived on time in Bangkok at 11:10PM. Now do I get a hotel room or spend the night at the airport? Checked availability at the airport hotel. No luck. Full. A local Thai tells me he'll take me to and pick me up in the morning from a hotel 25 minutes away for $35, or if I'd like, he'd take me to a massage parlor. This was most tempting as I felt like horse manure. I'd have to exchange money, exchange the money back, and if I fall asleep, I'll never wake up. Being so tired I'll probably miss my nine in the morning plane. I decided to stay at the airport.

I stretched out on the seats. Next thing I know, I'm surrounded by Thai's. They're heading to work in Saudi Arabia doing excavating. The guy I was talking to seemed amazed when he learned I was a tourist in Thailand four years ago and am now back touring again.

My thoughts go back to whether I should have headed for that massage. I thought of the last time I was in Thailand and had a massage. A full body massage and I mean full. It's two thirty in the morning and I'm wide awake. I dozed for a couple of hours. Now I'm having an orange juice with my last remaining baht. It's been 33 hours since I've left. I haven't really slept. Only dozed. I couldn't fall asleep. I caught Thai Airlines at nine for Kuala Lumpur (KL) Malaysia. After going through customs, I took a cab to Hotel Malaysia. Finally, I was able to take a shower. I met one group member, Heather, from New Zealand. I walked that evening in China Town. I had a chicken and rice dinner at one of the food stalls. Back at the hotel, we met Daphne, from Jersey in the Channel Islands off the coast of France.

It's now Saturday, November 18. We were supposed to take a ferry across the South China Sea to Kuching. However, the ferry workers were on strike. The plan now was to fly to Kuching on Sunday afternoon. We had a day to play. We hopped a bus to Port Kelang. Forty-five minutes later at Port Kelang, we walked over to the docks to see about catching a boat to the island. We learned we should go to Pula Ketam. It turned out to be a great day trip. We just walked around the area after an hour boat trip. Pula Ketam is built on stilted walkways. We saw the two-room homes and had a nice lunch of fried noodles and glop. Later, I had a kind of fried peanut butter pastry.

I was really tired when I got back to the hotel. I did not go with the rest to eat. Instead, I walked the market area around Chinatown. This was very interesting and very busy with stalls of food, clothes, usual tourist junk. Back at the hotel, I stripped off my clothes and fell into the bed for some long awaited Z's.

Started the next day, Sunday, by going to the train station to change reservations for Singapore, which is where I would be leaving from to go back home. Back at the hotel, I'm having coffee with Daphne when I see through the corner of my eye, a man approaching. He comes up and stands next to me. I figure it's some beggar and try ignoring him. Realizing he's staring, I look up. I was stunned! I couldn't believe it! It was my friend Crazy George, the Australian from my trip to Thailand in 1986! I said, "George, George!" and leaped out of my chair. We hugged each other, just amazed to see each other. George was headed to Indonesia on an adventure trip. The three of us spent the day shopping but mostly sitting outside, drinking beer and talking. Talk about a small world.

I caught a plane to Kuching at 6PM with a stopover in Singapore. Cleanest airport I've ever seen. Arriving in Kuching, we made it to Hotel Aurora.

The next day we caught a bus to Bako. Once here we took a motorized dugout canoe twenty-five minutes to Bako National Park. A beautiful tropical rain forest. We took the Jalan Lintang circular path lasting three hours. This was a deep Borneo jungle with lookouts over the open sea. A wild boar crossed our path and snorted away. Did not see any monkeys. The boat was going to pick us up at 3:10. It was 2:00 when we finished the trail. Just then a monsoon rain hit. It poured like I've never seen. We did not know if we would make it off the island. We started talking to another American who was there. He was working for Arco Oil in South

China. At about three-thirty the boatmen approach even though it was still raining. We had to climb over high rocks that had spine points and through knee-high water to get to the boat as water was at low tide. We were to catch the bus at five but didn't know if we would make it. The American offered us a ride back to Kuching in his rental car.

The next day we visited Semengok Wild Life Rehabilitation Center in Sarawak. The center is used mostly for orangutans. People who have injured or abandoned orangutans, monkeys or wild birds, have the animals brought here to learn how to live in the wild. From here we visited a "cat" museum and walked the city. Rained as usual. We ate at an Indian restaurant.

Woke up at five thirty in the morning to catch a nine in the morning plane to Sibu. From Sibu, we took a 2-hour river launch ride to Song. From Song a 2-hour dugout canoe journey to KH Jaksat Ng Liars Katisrar Song. Here Arnid, our guide, got out to get permission from the people for us to stay here. This is a most fascinating site. Twenty-four families living together in what is called a long-house. Like a row motel. High on stilts, a large verandah with single rooms behind curtains or doors. The living room and bedroom were the same. The bed is just a mat laid over the bamboo floor. Back room is the kitchen and storage. Then, back of all this is a squat toilet. I'll have constipation for two days-I hope. We'll be sleeping in the same room with the chief, his wife and kids. Very primitive lifestyle. No electricity. Open fire to cook over. We had dinner with the chief. We used our hands to eat. After we ate, the chief's wife and kids ate. Sleep was impossible. One of our mates, the good doctor from Belgium, snored like a cow all night. This kept the chief and boatman up also. Then the dogs barked, chickens clucked, pigs oinked and at five in the morning, the roosters took their turn.

We gathered in the canoe and headed downstream a bit. We got out and started hiking. Hiking in the jungles of Borneo, in the stream, up rocks, up hills. The Iban caught fish with a net as we walked. This was our lunch. Smoked pan fish. After the hike, we went further upstream to a more modern longhouse. Then came back for a rest. Little kids are all over me. They are feeling the hair on my arms. Dinner was-what else-rice with glop. However, this glop turned out to be curry beef and freshly-shot wild boar. Even a potato. Bathed, swam in the river before the night ceremony. An Iban, dressed up as a warrior and did a dance. We drank palm wine and more palm wine. We gave gifts to all 24 families. Then, we participated in the dancing.

I made friends with Richard, the chief's 15-year-old son. Our guide was interpreting for us. This was most interesting. Richard was on vacation from school. If he passed his examination, he will go back. If he didn't, he would hope to go to the logging camp to learn to be a mechanic. Since there is no area to walk around, the people just sit every night on the verandah. I was taken to the "souvenir" room. There I saw skulls. Human skulls. Not too long ago, these people were head-hunters. Wars with other tribes or passing adventurers were met with unwelcoming ways. I learned that most of these people have not been past the town of Sibu, which was four hours downstream. They don't know there is a world out there. I had little maps of the world. The older kids were most interested as I showed them where they lived and where I lived.

Again, I was conversing, or trying to, with Richard and his sixteen-year-old friend Sidi. Sidi quit school. Sidi also did not have a registration card. He was supposed to get one at age 12. He needed this card to be able to get a job. A Japanese logging firm was hiring the Iban men to cut the trees. In flying to Sibu, I saw the raping of the rain forest by these Japanese logging firms. Unfortunately, the Iban people did not realize the destruction they were causing their homeland.

I asked how Sidi was supposed to get a registration card. He needed to go to the city of Sibu, four hours down river, fill out a form, have his picture taken and that was that. I told Arnid to interpret that I would pay the cost to bring Sidi to Sibu and the cost involved to get his registration card. Sidi agreed to go and his Dad needed to come along for identification purposes.

Later that evening, Sidi came up to me and said in broken English "I appreciate what you do for me." I gave him a you're welcome smile.

I went to bed at one. Again, the Belgian snored, the dogs barked, the pigs grunted, chickens clucked and roosters roosted. Morning breakfast was rice with glop, what else. Sidi's Dad joined us but no Sidi. Sidi's Dad said he didn't want to go. Arnid and I went to see Sidi. Like a typical sixteen-year-old, he was still sleeping. We got him up and Arnid tried talking to Sidi but getting no response. Sidi's and my eyes connected. I was asking why when he was so excited last night about going, why the change of heart? His sad face just turned. We had to go, so we left Sidi behind. A village member was getting a ride by us to Sibu. I found out why Sidi didn't come with us. It showed me how these tribes living in remote areas of the world may think. Sidi's mother did not want her son and husband to go. She did not know what the outside world was, and was afraid that if her son and husband left for this place called Sibu, they would get lost and she would never see them again. Sidi's mom put the kibosh on the trip. Unfortunately, as the modern world encroaches on remote tribes, without any education or modern skills, tribes die off. Separated from their way of life, they are exploited for criminal activities. The movie, *The Emerald Forest*, is a good dramatization of what happens when the modern world takes over the primitive world.

Along the way to Sibu, we stopped at the Iban grave yard. When an Iban dies, all of his possessions are buried with him. At this site, there was a boat motor, dishes, radio.

Back in Sibu, we got a hotel room or what was called a hotel room. At least I was able to enjoy the three S's. Afterwards, Arnid and I walked around. Sitting, having a drink, we discussed that it was too bad about Sidi not coming. Also, what it would be like to bring an Iban to Sibu or Kuching. Show them what a television was. It would have been interesting. We thought of going back to the longhouse to get Sidi. Without a registration card, he can not travel or get work. Sidi had said he didn't want to stay at the longhouse. He will have to stay there and be a farmer like his Dad.

We went to an Islamic restaurant. I had a great meal. A Muertabak. It's a dough with chicken and vegetables fried up like a giant omelet. Went to bed at ten.

Woke up at eight. It was great to get a good night's sleep. We don't have to leave until one thirty, so I strolled the city. I can't find anyplace to get a normal breakfast. I could get juice, coffee, eggs and bacon for about 80 cents American. We caught a plane to Miri. Miri is an oil town with not much to see. Arnid and I went to dinner. Noodles with chicken and vegetables. Very good, costing only $2M or 75 cents. Arnid and I strolled the streets. Miri is famous for prostitution. Arnid and I went to three different places of ill repute. The girls sit outside their room as you walk down the hall. You view the ladies and pick one out. Cost for a quickie is $30M or $11 American. Arnid is talking to one of the girls who was afraid of me as she thought Europeans were too "big." I should be so lucky. Not indulging, we went and had a drink and listened to a soft rock band. Very nice. I went to bed about eleven.

Today is Sunday. We went to see the Niah Caves. Very interesting place. Locals climb ropes to the top of the caves to raid bird nests for bird drop soup. Bird drop soup is bird saliva. Sounds gross but it is a delicacy for locals. The cave is inhabited by swiftlets and bats. As darkness sets in, hundreds of swiftlets fly into the caves. Amazing sights. The bats fly out for their nightly feeding.

Finally, I had a decent breakfast the next morning. Cheese omelet, potatoes, toast, and coffee. We caught a plane to Sabah. Then bussed up to Kinabalu National Park. We took in a slide show of the mountain trek we were going to do up Mt. Kinabulu. We received a briefing by Arnid. The hike does not seem as tough as I thought. It will be like climbing a lot of stairs. I had a great dinner. Sirloin steak with mushroom gravy, salad and fries. Staying with Arnid tonight rather than a cabin with the others. I don't need to hear the Belgian snore.

It's the 28th of November when we start our climb up Mt. Kinabalu. Our goal is to get to Low's Point at 13,455 feet. At 11,000 feet we would stop for the night at Lamban Rata-a lodge in the clouds. I was right. The climb was like climbing stairs. Stairs and more stairs. Tough going, but I felt good. At the seven rest stops, I had water and was able to get my composure back quite easily. The climb never stopped. Up and up. Finally around two, five hours later, I reached the hut. Cold and wet, but feeling all right. I took a hot shower. Then I had some hot chicken soup. We had a room where all six of us stayed. A discussion on the climb to the summit was held. We had to wake up at two in the morning to be ready to leave by three to reach the summit by sunrise.

Went to bed at eight after a dinner of sweet and sour chicken. I worried how I would feel at two in the morning. Awake at midnight as Mark was snoring again. Woke him up at one to shut him up. I woke up and eager to go at two. I had some toast and tea before starting off.

Traveling in the dark with nothing but a flashlight, we climbed and climbed. Steeper than the day before.

We were above the tree line. Sheer rock faces where at times we had to use ropes. I was climbing in the dark, on my own, as some climbers were faster, some slower.

I was hiking with Malaysians, then Australians for a while. My hands started to get cold. Very cold. Numb. I could not see how much further as the darkness and sheer rock face prevented a clear view. I just kept climbing. Very slowly. I had to stop to warm my hands. Mark came by and offered me his warm gloves. Mine were wet from sweat. After some warm up, I continued the climb. The air is thin and the going is slow. Finally, I saw the summit. Very steep climb to reach it. Made it. Signed the book at 6:05 in the morning. I got my picture taken with the sign marking the reaching of Low's Point. I tried taking pictures, but my hands were frozen. The night climb was beautiful with a star-filled sky. After the sunrise, I visited with the climbers and started back down. Mark gave me his gloves again as my hands were freezing. Going down was hard on my knees as the climb down, like the climb up, was steep. Seeing what I climbed up, now that it was light, shocked me. Shocked, that I was able to actually climb up the steep mountain. Good thing I couldn't see the climb. I may not have done it. Staggered back to the complex at 11,000 feet about two hours later, cold and wet. I dried off and changed clothes. I had French toast and coffee. Slept half an hour before the final descent at ten. Traveled the final part with Mark, Paulette, Arnid, and the mountain guide. It was painful. My right knee gave out. It hurt like hell. I had to take two small steps instead of one large one. Mark was having the same trouble. Climbing down, down, down in agony. Really slow going. What should have taken no more than three hours to get down, took over three and a half. I was hurting. I got a cabin at the park, showered and laid down. This was the medicine. I felt terrific. What a feeling of accomplishment. This last day's climb was hell. Three hours up to the summit, two hours back to the lodge at 11,000 feet. Three and a half hours back to base. Eight and a half hours. Seeing the path we took up as we came down made my little group wonder how we achieved this climb. I realized this wasn't Mount Everest, with ropes, ice axes, oxygen, and such. But for me, a working stiff, it was my own adventure. My own feeling of accomplishment. My triumph. I had a great tasting cashew nut chicken dinner and went to bed at eight.

It was the last day of November, a Thursday, as we traveled to the city of Kota Kinabulu and stayed at the fancy hotel Shangri-La. We took a boat out to an island. We laid out on the white sand beach, swam and snorkeled in the warm China Sea. The girls tanned topless which seemed to bother Arnid. Some custom about nudity in public places. Back at town for evening stroll and shopping. Fun and cheap. Back at hotel, I had some great ice cream and listened to music.

Now the hard part. I had to say good-bye to Arnid. I told him we'd meet again in America. Hopefully, our idea of bringing Richard-the Iban child to America can become a reality. We hugged to bid farewell to a new and hopefully continuing friendship. This would be the start of the good-byes which are always difficult. You are thrown together with strangers for a short time. You share an experience, a challenge that brings a closeness that only travelers can know. It would not matter that we would not see one another again, but enjoyed an experience with good people from different parts of the world. I said good-bye to Marc and Paulette. I caught a plane to Kuala Lumpur. What we thought was a direct flight turned out to be an all afternoon journey as we had to stopover in Singapore. In KL, I took a cab to Hotel Malay to drop off the girls. I than cabbed over to the Station Hotel, located, where else, the train station. I did this so I could be there to catch the 7:30AM train to Singapore. What a dump, but at least it had air conditioning. I walked over to meet the girls for dinner. After a meal of chicken rice type soup and a peanut pancake-I think that's what I ate-I said good-bye to the girls and went shopping. I walked back to Station Hotel, bed by eleven.

Early Saturday morning, I wake up at six. I ate an egg and cheese sandwich with orange juice for breakfast. Then at 7:30 I caught the 7:30 express train to Singapore. No problems. I traveled in the first class car. Very nice. Air conditioned and I had a window seat. Later, I went to have lunch. I sat with two teenage girls. My order was the chicken curry. The girls said I should eat with the spoon and not the fork. Chit-chatted with the youngins. Typical teenagers who hang out at the mall on weekends. I told them the only difference I notice on my travels is the different language on the Coca-Cola bottles.

Plush green landscapes from KL to Singapore. The rains keep everything growing.

I went through customs, then took a cab to Hotel Grand Central. I was enjoying my trip in style. This was a fancy hotel. I took a nice, long, hot shower. I noticed some business cards from some fine lady entrepreneurs had been slipped under my door. Called Heather who was staying at the Y. We met at the Lucky Plaza Shopping Center. Miles of high rise shopping centers and all are packed with people. Bargaining is the way of buying things. We went to an open market area for dinner where there were a bunch of food vendors. Fresh fish, still alive until cooked. I had another chicken Muertaback. Love those things. We went people watching which is always great fun as there are masses of people to watch.

Sunday came which was my last full day. I shopped till I dropped. I bought a tape cassette player and a beautiful suede leather winter jacket. It was getting late so I headed to the airport at seven thirty for my all night vigil as my plane does not leave until six forty-five in the morning. I decided to spend the night at the airport rather than the hotel as the plane was leaving so early. I didn't want to have to wake before the sun and rush to the airport. Plus, I would save money and have an adventure of staying in what was a nice airport. The hours passed. It's now one thirty in the morning. I'm listening to tunes on my new cassette player. I'm not tired yet. I'll need to stay awake to adjust to Minneapolis time which is 11:30am. It worked coming here. I avoided jet lag. I hope I can do the same again. Now it's 8am and I stayed awake all night. The stomach started talking to me as my last meal was at 5:30pm. At the time, I didn't even think when my next meal would be. The trouble was, instead of sleeping, I was awake all night. Now I just finished breakfast, fourteen hours after my last meal. Time to go through customs and all and board the plane. Getting settled on the plane, I get another grab bag. Let's see what I got. Oh, good. Another mask. I get sleeping socks which I will use as I'm not wearing any. Breakfast was a cheese omelet with breakfast steak, potatoes, blueberry muffin, fresh fruit and an apple danish. The movie, which I already saw, is *Honey I Shrunk the Kids*. Anyway, I must stay awake to adjust to Minneapolis time which is now 6pm. We make a stop in Tokyo some five and a half hours after leaving Singapore. I will go to sleep, hopefully, after leaving Tokyo as it will be about 11pm Minneapolis time. Just finished watching the movie. I've been up now for twenty seven hours. One and a half hours till Tokyo. I'll have a tomato juice then take a nap. A businessman is in front of me sleeping with his tie on. Can't they ever leave the office? A woman kitty corner is polishing her nails while a Japanese girl across from me has been covered up like a cocoon from the start. I'm sure there's a body under those blankets.

Arrived Tokyo. We had to get off the plane to walk over to another gate to get back on. Plane leaving at 3pm Tokyo time. I've been up 30 hours sans a 45 minute wink coming in. What's this? Another goodie bag? I'm going to have my own collection of Lone Ranger costumes with all the masks. Dinner came which was a not a too bad steak. Once again, no one is sitting next to me.

I'm going to stretch out for Z's. Got about five hours shut-eye. No sound sleep though. Trip's about over. A very good one. Only one more decision left to make. I think I'll have the blueberry pancakes.

CHAPTER 9

▼

AMAZON: ADVENTURE BEFORE THE ADVENTURE

It's been four years since my last adventure trip. Four years since Borneo. There was a good reason for this. I became a parent. A single parent as I became a foster parent. This did not stop the trips. Just the adventure trips I was used to. However, since David was 12 years old, I just altered the adventures. No matter what your situation is, you can make an adventure. So it was off on a cruise to the Bahamas. I had never been on a cruise, so David and I hit Disney World and a cruise. Like any corporate slave, I had some money to invest. When some friends invited me to their time-share unit in Aruba, I bought one. I started traveling the luxurious way to places like Lake Tahoe and Puerto Rico. However, back at work I had more responsibilities. Other things changed. David moved out. Also, a relationship I had soured. My job was making me a working stiff. The cure for all this was an adventure trip. It was time to find an adventure.

Unfortunately, I couldn't take a lot of extended time. That meant no big international adventure. I started reading adventure trip materials again. I came up with what sounded great. The Amazon. A week-long trip from Saturday to Saturday. Departure in March so I could get out of the Minnesota winter. The cost was a bit high, but included round-trip airfare from Miami. Plus, we would be staying in lodges as opposed to tent camping. I signed up. The trip would only be on the Peruvian side of the Amazon, but it looked like a full week of things to do and see.

Even though this trip would not be a physically demanding trip as my others were, I still started running and working out in preparation for the trip. My innoculations were still in effect, so I didn't get any new ones. Not even a gamma globulin.

Saturday rolled around. As usual, the adventure began before the actual trip. Being the cheap jerk I am, I was able to obtain a TWA friend and family ticket for $49 round trip from Minneapolis to Miami. I was to meet the group in Miami. The Faucett flight was leaving Miami at 6pm for Iquitos. I was to arrive in Miami at one in the afternoon, making a connection in St. Louis on TWA. The ticket I had was standby. I had called previously and was told I had a good chance. Again, I asked at the Minneapolis check-in about the availability for getting on the flight from St. Louis to Miami. I was told that chances looked pretty good and I had no problem getting on the Minneapolis to St. Louis flight. However, I did not make it on the St. Louis to Miami flight. It was full. Panic time. The next flight to Miami would have me arrive at 4:45. Still enough time. However, I found out that plane could be full. There was one seat left. $500. I checked other airlines. No better deals. What to do? What to do? Out came the credit card. So instead of saving $300, I was out $500. I left a voice mail with the tour group of a change in arrival time.

I arrived in Miami close to five in the afternoon. One hour to get to Faucett Airlines. The Miami Airport is huge, so I would have to hustle. Getting of the plane, I noticed a gentleman holding a placard with my name. I introduced myself. He was not a happy camper. You might say he was pissed. "The plane's waiting for you. We have to hurry."

"I thought it wasn't leaving till 6. I have an hour."

"Everybody is on the plane. It's leaving at 5."

Shit. These third world airlines. Set their own schedule daily. We ran across the airport. One bag on my back. I'm dripping with sweat. We come to the security check area. Another problem. My ticket was waiting for me at the gate. You needed a ticket to pass through security. The Spanish language started flying. The escort explaining the situation. The security person not allowing me through. Then to top it off, as my camping bag goes through x-ray, my camping knife is noticed. More Espanol. Arguments going left and right. Finally, as a guard starts approaching, the escort and I just pass through and leave them behind. I'm soaked from sweat. The plane is still there. The gate agent greets me, says "Relax", and hands me a ticket. "You'll like the seat", she said. That I did. I had a business class seat with no one next to me. I was handed a glass of champagne and escargot. I used the napkins to wipe the sweat. I finally cooled down and relaxed. I looked around for other group members but didn't see anyone. They were back in the cheap seats. I stretched out, ate, relaxed, and caught a nap on my way to Iquitos, Peru. Upon arrival, I was one of the first through customs. I still had not met any member of the group. As people were coming through customs, I approached what looked to be a "groupie". They all thought I was left behind in Miami. I didn't want to tell them I flew in luxury.

Iquitos is a frontier city on the banks of the Amazon river. It was dark and raining when we arrived. We just headed to a hotel.

"Under a canopy of trees a hundred feet tall, the rain forest shelters an astonishing exuberance of plant and animal life. Amidst the wondrous beauty and diversity of the forest, observe firsthand the complex interactions of this ecosystem. Also learn how the indigenous people utilize the resources of the forest for food, shelter and medicines; and how the pressures of population are affecting the environment. Ascend into the uncharted world of the forest canopy on the existing canopy walkway, a suspended system of aerial footpaths and stairways providing an unparalleled view across the roof of the forest." Alas, my next adventure was to begin.

After breakfast in the hotel, we had a short bus ride through the city of Iquitos and a look at the Amazon River. Here we boarded a thatch-roofed motor launch for a 50-mile journey down the Mighty Amazon to Explorama Lodge. Along the way we would pass numerous islands, some several miles long, observing the way of life of the "Riberenos" river people with their thatch-roofed dwellings and dugout canoes. The river often exceeds two miles in width. Floating logs make for some quick boating maneuvers. The lodge is located deep in the rain forest. Much care went into preserving the surroundings. Plank walkways led to a dining hall, bar, sitting area, bathrooms (pit style), showers (cold), and bedrooms-motel hallway style. This would be luxury from the trips I had been used to. After settling in and a buffet lunch, we explored the Bushmaster Trail. Very lush jungle trail where we learned about the many plants and animal species encountered along the way, such as medicinal herbs, leaf-cutter ants-which I was very familiar with-poison dart frogs, tarantulas, and how each fits into the complex system. The rain forest may have the cures for most medical problems, yet not enough is being done to protect the rainforests.

After dinner, the locals made music and the dancing began. We encountered an American doctor living here. Story goes, she was on a similar tour as us. She was about to leave when she was summoned to help a local child who was bitten by a snake. She decided to stay. Closed her practice in Wisconsin and set up shop here in this remote area. Also here at this time was a fraternal group based in Northern Minnesota who held fund-raisers to get money to build, first the clinic, now an addition. The doctor runs the clinic on her own. The people here are very poor-in a monetary way. They mostly farm. When they have enough of a crop or whatever they make, some of the family catch a river taxi to Iquitos where they may spend a week and sell their goods.

The bar had beers. What could be better? The nice evening ended early as I was tired from the long day.

Awakening at dawn to a forest alive with unforgettable sights and sounds as we heard and saw toucans, brightly colored macaws, and walking stick insects. After breakfast, we set out by small launch to observe the elusive freshwater pink dolphin. They came close to our boat, but not close enough to touch. We explored little tributaries to see many birds and a monkey. There are many tributaries in the Amazon. The Amazon itself is the largest river system in the world. Over two-thirds of all the fresh water on earth is found within the Amazon Basin. There are over 1,100 tributaries, some over 1,000 miles long.

We stopped at a village. Nothing exciting here except a pet sloth that we all took turns holding for pictures.

Back at the lodge for dinner, the meals were served buffet-style. Always some chicken, beef, or fish on the menu, along with fresh vegetables.

As night settles in, we walk the thatched wooden walkways that link the buildings. There is no electricity; light is provided by kerosene lamps. Open half-wall rooms lets in the sounds of the birds and animals. Two beds in each room covered by mosquito netting.

After breakfast the following day, we depart by boat to Explore Napo Lodge. After going about seven miles, the Amazon is joined by the Napo River, the largest of the Peruvian tributaries. Here the first European, Francisco de Orellana, encountered the Amazon River in 1541. Turning up the Napo, going about 40 miles, we get to the Sucusari River, a serpentine dark-water tributary where the rustic dormitory-style Explore Napo Camp is located. The camp is nestled in a beautiful spot amidst the remote rain forest on the boundary of the Amazon Biosphere Reserve. The Reserve contains 250,000 acres of primary rain forest preserved for scientific study and educational exploration. The lodge is open air with dormitory-style sleeping arrangements with mats along the floor covered with mosquito netting.

After lunch we take a trail through the immense trees of the forest. The terrain is more hilly and we see many different plants and animal species. Later on we go looking for caiman and the strange-looking hoatzin. A big ugly bird most closely related to the cuckoo. They inhabit vegetation along the blackwater lakes of the Napo Region and build their nests over-hanging the water. Here, also, in these blackwaters are giant victoria water lilies whose leaves can exceed seven feet in diameter and support the weight of a child.

Not too much to do in the evening. I sit and read. Catch an early Z.

The next morning, we follow a trail deeper into the rain forest. The feeling of being here in the depths of the Amazon rain forest is very satisfying. We reach the ACEER (Amazon Center for the Environmental Education and Research). We encounter motel style rooms again. An American student is living here doing a graduate paper on frogs. Kind of a lonely, desolate area to study in. We take a night walk after dinner to learn about the rain forest's nocturnal inhabitants, such as bats, amphibians, and interesting insects. Surprisingly, mosquitoes are not a serious problem in the Amazon. I have more of a problem with them at home. The ACEER serves as a research base for scientists from all over the globe. It is a very interesting place out here in nowhere. I look forward to tomorrow when I'll see the grand canopy walkway.

So I did. What a grand sight to see. A short walk through arboreal giants brings you to a natural ridge and the initial climb. A series of wooden stairways. A footpath, suspended among the trees on both rope and cable supports, extends through the delicate green shadows and disappear into the foliage of yet a higher tree over 100 yards away. The first steps are scary. Very slow going for me. The footpaths sway and some have steep climbs to the next walkway. The walkway goes up over 100 feet high. Being in and above the trees enables scientists to study this unexplored world where in the branches of a single tree, over 2,000 epiphytic plants may cling and hundreds of insect species may be found, 80% as yet unknown to science. Reaching the top and looking over the trees is amazing. Also, amazing is the feat of engineering that is the canopy walkway. The walkway is strong, safe and built with no stress on the trees and ecosystem. This was a real treat to see.

I descend from the treetops for lunch and a short rest. In the afternoon, we follow the Medicine Trail, learning about the plants and their uses in the Indian's pharmacopoeia.

The couple of days here at the ACEER were truly worthwhile. To see an area of study, deep in the rain forest brings hope that some new discovery may be made. We head back to Explornapo Camp, board boats for the return to Explorama Lodge. The three and a half hour trip provides more opportunities to observe local life on the river. Big families were a sign of prestige. Since there is no electricity, darkness sets in and there is nothing much else to do.

However, with the world encroaching on what used to be primitive river people, the larger families will suffer. They do not have the education needed to survive. Children are sent to schools in Iquitos and leave their families behind. Climbing into a typical house I observed the simple lifestyle. I thought if only the river people could be left alone.

Back at the lodge, my guide, Julio and I went canoeing. These dugout canoes don't seem as sturdy as the canoes back home. Smaller and lower in the water made the short rapids exciting. Julio drew a map of the area we traveled during our time in the Amazon on a canoe paddle for me. What a great souvenir!

It's Saturday, our last day. We make an early departure from the lodge. Hang around Iquitos until our evening flight on Faucett Airlines. I'm able to take my canoe paddle on the plane. Since I have a window seat, I lay the paddle along the wall. Everything is fine until I find out we have to exchange planes in Lima. It's after midnight. We get a special escort to take us through the airport, get through customs and wait in the departure area. Upon going through the door to the tarmac to board the plane, I'm stopped by an official. He will not let me bring the paddle on the plane. I must check it. The Spanish started flowing as I started bitching. Argument didn't last long as I lost and had to check the paddle.

Made it to Miami. Canoe paddle made it also. I still had to see if my TWA pass would work to get me home. I needed to save some money. It did.

A short adventure such as this can appeal to a vast majority. Men, women, senior citizen, or teen. For the working stiff, it's a lot of adventure in just a week's time. Have you been working so hard that you didn't notice your child has grown into a teen? Bring your teen and have some bonding. This trip was no bus tour by any means but a mild adventure that can be done by anyone able to walk. There were two seventy something women on this trip. They were unable to do the canopy walkway so instead, took their own nature hike.

I learned to plan ahead. If I would have left a day early, I could play around with the cheap stand-by tickets I was using. However, since this was not my own trip on my own time, I had to be at a certain place at a certain time. I had not allowed myself the luxury of preventing a glitch and having an alternative. Therefore, when you have to be someplace at some certain time, don't try to be cheap. Instead, try to find the best way at the best price to get to your needed location.

CHAPTER *10*

▼

SOUTHEAST ASIA: CHOOSING A TRAVELING COMPANION

For years I had been thinking of taking an adventure that I would plan. I would go alone or with a companion. No adventure group. It could possibly be my last real adventure. I'm nearing 50 years old. I first started my adventures by hitchhiking when I was 22. I cannot climb mountains anymore like Mount Kinabalu in Borneo or cross the great rain forests like the Darien Gap.

I am a working stiff mired in the corporate world. I make a comfortable living. I enjoy camping in the summer and a winter week getaway to Aruba. Occasional trips to Las Vegas content me now as opposed to the rigors of the adventure trips. Looking back, it was a great choice. I've learned a lot about people, ways of life, met friends and saw some of the world. I've had a fun, adventurous past twenty-five years. However, I'm not dead yet. It's off again. It's time for another adventure.

The first question of planning a trip is where to go. This can be determined by how much money one is willing to spend. Being the cheap guy that I am, I turn to my frequent flyer tickets. I don't fly for my job anymore. However, I do have enough frequent flyer miles for a last adventure. They will be expiring so I need to go now. Deciding where to go again depends on where Northwest Airlines flies. That leaves Southeast Asia. Since I had been to Thailand before, what could I do for what may be my final adventure? To the library I would go. This would take a lot of research on my part. Should I go alone or take my nephew who had expressed an interest. We had a great time together when I took him on a camping expedition up to Churchill, Canada for a high school graduation present. However, he went and got himself married. That took care of him. I decided to write the trip first, find a traveling companion second and ask the boss for time off third. I was in no real hurry so occasionally I went to the library. Over the course of two years, did the trip actually get put on paper and an actual plan started to progress. It was postponed for a year due to new responsibilities at work. I finally decided to travel from Bangkok to Malaysia to Singapore by way of the train with stops to islands and rain forests. I studied train schedules, travel times, lengths of intended stays, etc. I determined I would need 21 days to do the trip. I mentioned to my boss what I was working on and at the time she didn't seem concerned. Now to find someone to go with. A companion can make or break a trip. Never would I go with a stranger from say a bulletin board at the University. Problem was all my friends were married, and always thought I was kind of a nut anyway for these travels I did. So I would have to find an acquaintance. I was taking a graduate class at the University of Minnesota on adventure education (I got a B) when I found out a friend of my nephew's was taking classes. I knew Jason. He was a continuing student getting different degrees. He seemed interested but couldn't commit at the time. I heard a friend of my sister's did some "adventure" travel. A couple of inquiries later, we got together to discuss. I knew Nancy as we had gone out a couple of times years ago. She knew the rigors of this kind of travel. She knew she may not have a daily bath let alone know where she might sleep each night. This was part of the adventure. It was set. Now I had to work on the dates for the trip and the time off. Damn Northwest Airlines and their frequent flyer program. I gave them 30 different dates for travel. I even said I would fly into Singapore and out of Bangkok or vice-versa-whatever. I was as flexible as I could be and this was five months before my intended departure date. To get anything, I had to cut five days from my trip. After getting on wait lists and pestering, I got what I needed within one day.

Problem. My boss said I could only have two weeks in a row-not three. I had a total of twenty two days between vacation and personal time off. So the twenty one days I needed-one day was a holiday-was not anything I didn't have coming. It was that it would be all at once. Nancy was having a problem but she said she could get the time off. I had a decision to make. I continued with the plans for the trip. I would confront my boss again. I decided I was going on the trip. If it meant my job, so be it. I had never even taken a sick day in my twelve years with the company. There was no reason why I should not be able to go. During my yearly review, I was getting good comments. However, it now came time for me to raise the issue. I could feel for my boss on the hardship it would have on the team. However, anytime I took a vacation, I would see that someone covered for me. Through a good discussion, my boss approved the trip. I was a happy man.

Now the planning got more meaningful. The trip I planned for the past two years was going to happen. I had the travel dates, I had the travel companion, I was ready to go. This was my plan.

Day 1-3: Arrive Bangkok: See temples, floating market and city life.

Day 4-6: Train to Surat Thani-Boat to Koh Samui. Beautiful island is very much a travelers center. Third largest island in Thailand. Beautiful beaches and scenic waterfalls. A stay in Bo Phut will be less crowded.

Day 7-8: Surat Thani to Hat Yai/Thale Ban National Park. Six hour train ride. Undisturbed rain forest. Varied wildlife includes Bat Hawk,

Peregrine falcon, monkeys, barking frogs. Accommodations in lakeside bungalows.

Day 9-12: Hat Yai to Khota Bharu (station is Wakaf Bharu). Boat from Khota Bharu via of Kuala Beset to Perhentian Islands. Islands possess everything that tropical islands should possess such as idyllic white beaches, green waters, dense rain forests criss-crossed by trails. Coral reefs, brilliant sunsets, snorkeling. Paradise is the appropriate word.

Day 13-16: Pasir Mas to Jerantut (six hours): Night in Jerantut. Shared taxi or bus to boat to Taman Negara Park. Minor rapids. Prime National Park. Enormous expanse of lush jungle. Orang Asil settlements. Accommodations at Kuala Tahan. Almost impenetrable forest with multitude of bird and animal life including eagles, osprey, kingfisher, tiger, elephant, tapir, civet cat and barking deer.

Day 16-18: Jerantut to Gemas to Kuala Lumpur. See capital city including Indian temple, street vendors and more.

Day 19-21: Kuala Lumpur to Singapore. Shop till you drop. Shop the stores with bargains galore. Depart to home.

The final days of work had me going like a mad man trying to get everything done. I still needed to show others how to do my work. It was hard to get excited about the trip with what work I needed to finish. Finally, the last day of work. The end of the day finally came. I left the office, got in my car, and just sat there. I gave a big sigh of relief. I sat there savoring the moment.

Saturday. Final day. I get everything done. Stop the mail, finalize money, pay bills, give key to neighbor, and repack. Spent a couple of hours at friends, then started to tire.

I went home and to bed at eleven. I had no trouble falling asleep. I got a good night's sleep, which was probably my last for some time. Arriving at the airport early, I was going to try to upgrade my coach seat to business class. On the free ticket I was using, I couldn't upgrade even by paying cash. So much for getting to the airport early.

There were three seats in our row. Nancy had the window, I with the aisle. Now everybody's nightmare. Would there be someone assigned to the middle seat? If so, would their body size overflow onto our space? Did I have to look forward to twelve hours of airplane seating torture? People started coming down the aisle, no please, not him. Keep on going. That's right, pass us by. What's this? A woman slowing down. A Hong Kongish-type lady took the middle seat. At least she was small. Still, the twelve hour flight to Narita will not be fun.

Happy Gilmore. It's relaxing when you can settle in and watch a movie to help pass the time. *Happy Gilmore*. I propped up the pillow, cuddled under the blanket, got situated to watch the movie. *Happy Gilmore*. That was the movie? Damn, I'll read instead.

It never got dark outside. We headed west from Minneapolis, crossed the date line and now were heading east.

It's 3:15am, Minneapolis time. Time for my body clock to get screwed up. Arrived in Tokyo just to change planes for the final leg to Bangkok. I'm getting punchy. It's five hours forty minutes to Bangkok. I'll get comfortable. It's kind of relaxing when you can settle in and watch a movie to help pass the time. I propped up the pillow, cuddled under the blanket, and got situated. *Cutthroat Island*. This was the movie. I brought out the book.

Arrived in Bangkok at eleven at night. We got through customs, exchanged money, and here we were. Hoards of Thai's offering to help. Help take your money from you. We had a destination. A motel in the Banglampho area. This was the traveler's Mecca of cheap hotels. We had a room for 250 baht or $10. The room has a fan, squat toilet, drip shower and a barking dog. If we wanted toilet paper, it would be 5 baht more. Where was that Holiday Inn?

Didn't sleep well. Only dozed for four hours. I decided to upgrade the room. We found another hotel for twice the price-$20. For this, we got an air-conditioned room, a bed with sheets and a sit-down, flush toilet. Luxury for only $10 more.

A day for sight-seeing. Here's what can happen when you use personal transportation. We got in a tic-tic cab. He would be our tour guide. He took us to a couple of temples. Along the way he took us to retail outlets. He said he would get gas coupons from the store if he would bring customers there. We only went to one. When he tried taking us to another store, we said no. He said out. That was fine with us. We walked. We walked some more. Finally, made it back to the hotel where we took a nap. Woke up and went to dinner. We ended up at a restaurant with local music. I had fried rice with chicken.

Slept a little better that night. Ate a cheese omelet, toast and coffee for breakfast. How American. We hopped on a boat taxi to Wat Pho. Beautiful area of temples. I was blessed by a monk priest and given a good luck journey bracelet. This Wat, or temple, has an enormous leaning Buddha. A school was located here. The students were giving shoulder massages. I indulged. Another trick of the tuk-tuk drivers, is to tell you certain temples are closed. They do this in hopes you will go with them to the "open" sights. A real scam.

We went to the Grand Palace. This was supposed to be "closed." There was a strict dress code here. I had to put on a long pair of pants that they supplied. I had to give up my passport for security to make sure I brought the pants back. After the palace, we stopped for some fried noodles with chicken. Not much happening tonight so we planned for tomorrow. It is so hot that just walking outside causes me to sweat. The weather wears on you. Glad we still have the air-conditioned room, even if we are paying $20 a night. This area of Banglamphu along Khao San Road has all kinds of guest houses from dorm rooms for a couple of bucks upward. A cab drops off a load of back-packers. They scout around for a place to crash. It's a throw-back to the sixties for me. Not a lot of Americans. A wide range of nations are represented along this street. Europeans have an easier time with this type of nomadic travel. Places are closer and flights are less costly to get. Some tour around for months. It's a way of life for some to enjoy while they are young. Single travelers team up with others if they are going in the same direction. They might even team up to do a side trip like doing a hill-tribe trek. They would become instant friends, enjoy a short adventure together, and then good-bye. A forever memory with another wanderer named-well whatever it was, he was fun to be with and we had a great time.

The next day we took the river taxi down to the fancy hotels and Riverplace Shopping Center. Very nice resorts and you pay the price. I saw a teak rice barge replica I wanted to buy. Since I traveled on a rice barge when I was in Thailand previously, it brought back memories. Price was fair at 6,000 baht or $240. I would have bought it but wouldn't have been able to carry it. So instead, I bought some silk boxers.

We had the day to pass as the bus we were to catch wasn't leaving until 5:30pm. Nancy went her way, I went mine. We later met for dinner where we split a plate of rice with chicken. I'm hardly eating and I'm not feeling hungry. I haven't had a bowel movement in four days.

Time to catch the bus. By traveling overnight we would save 500 baht by not paying for a hotel. We were headed to Surat Thani, an eleven hour ride. From Surat Thani, another hour bus ride to the pier. We were headed to the Island of Koh Samui which was two and a half hours by ferry.

On the ferry we are surrounded by bungalow owners trying to get us to stay with them. One sounds nice. We'll give it a look.

It's a hideaway. Little one room cottages. Ours has a deck overlooking the water. A semi-flush toilet with shower. All for 120 baht or $4.90. Very peaceful. Too peaceful. There is nothing else around. Our staying here another night will depend on other's staying here and we can strike up a friendship. Otherwise, it's off to a place with more activity. We're staying on the northern part of the island. At night we sat on the beach and watched sand crabs. I finished reading my book while Nancy talked with other travelers who were staying at the Banta resort. Rain storm that night. The next morning, we were told the husband from the "resort" would drive us to the area of Naton. About 10 am, however, all hell broke loose. A family cab driver friend of the resort owner was having coffee with the hung-over owner. Since it was 8 am, I asked for the cost of a ride to Naton. He said 100 baht. We were being ripped off. Tops should have been 40 baht. We told him no thanks. Asked the husband owner about the ride at 10 am that the Mrs. said he would do. He was still hung-over and said no. We packed our bags and walked on the porch. He came and locked the room door so we couldn't get back in. The two Swedes that Nancy was talking with last night were also going to Naton. Like us, they were told the husband would take them. It was now 10:15. They started arguing with the old man. The husband was being a real jerk. Now the Australians, who Nancy also talked to last night, were in on the fracas. They were going to stay longer. They had rented a motor bike from this place for 24 hours and wanted the bike for ten more minutes. The husband said no. We all said fuck this place, shouted more obscenities to the old man, and started hiking out. Walking out along the dirt road, husband came by in the truck. We stayed in the road. He was going to run us down. We got out of the way. At the main road, we decided to head to a place that Magnus found the previous day. We bargained with a taxi and ended up at the Weekender Villa. Cost was 100 baht or $4 for the night. Right on the water. Porch, two beds, fan and a toilet you throw water in to flush. You are your own flusher.

We had lunch with our new found friends, the Swedes and Australians. Being a working stiff, I was lucky to get these three weeks off to do my wanderlust travel. Here, these two couples were out for a year. How could they do this? The Aussie's company downsized. He was given a big severance with a non-compete clause of two years. The Swedes also lost their jobs. So off they went. Most nomad travelers came to Southeast Asia as it's so affordable. Transportation, food, lodging can be very cheap if you want to do budget travel. I can get a big dinner of rice and chicken for $1.

Being on the go, you only eat two meals a day. Therefore, food and drink is about $5 per day. A budget room can run from $4 to $9. I went to Bangkok to Surat Tani, an eleven hour bus ride for $15 which was on an upgraded bus. From Nepal to India, Thailand, Malaysia, Indonesia, and Vietnam, the nomad traveler, this sub-culture of adventurers, come vagabonding along. Europe is expensive and the US is not affordable or easy to get around. Seeing backpackers is the norm here. Think about the last time you saw a backpacker riding public transportation.

Before we decided on the Weekender Villa, we looked at a room at the adjacent villa. More deluxe with two beds, flush toilet, central air, wrap-around deck and overlooking the water for $25. So why am I staying in a place with less conveniences for $4. I can well afford the $25 room. When doing budget travel, you get a budget traveler's mindset. I was going to buy a T-shirt. The asking price was 180B or $7. I put the T-shirt down and started to walk away. The price was now 150B or $6. I was a jerk as I did offer 120B but was refused. Again, it's the mindset of budget travel.

I've always traveled with adventure groups. You pay the price and the itinerary is planned. Now, I pay as I go and plan the next legs of the trip as I go. I have to make the arrangements. Plans don't go as originally planned. From here to Ko Samui, I had planned to go to Hat Yai onto Thale National Park. I discovered the park would be hard to come by. A lot of time would have been spent on local buses. I didn't have the time. Also, seeing the Perhentian Islands was now out. Seeing this island was enough and again, the time was a factor. I didn't have six months or a year to travel where time didn't matter for getting to a place. I figure my days in travel days. We decided to stay an extra day where we were and leave on Monday.

As the six of us conversed over lunch, we laughed at the morning's happening. We wished we could be back at Banta Lodge when the wife comes back and finds us all gone. Since it started to rain, we planned the next day's activities. That night we had great fun, chatting, drinking, playing cards with the Aussies, Len and Anne, along with the Swedes, Magnus and Lota. One learns a lot from other travelers' experiences. You learn what to be careful of. For instance, if you have your pack on top of a flat bed truck, taxi, or a bus, the "luggage watcher" may go through yours. Locks don't help as they will pry the zipper. If others see that you are sleeping, they will reach under your seat or crawl under to get your bag if you have it at your feet.

The next day, Sunday, we rented a motor bike to travel to a waterfall. We hiked up to a waterfall and then were headed down another path to a different waterfall. As we rounded a bend, we came upon an embarrassing and startling scene. Two local Thais were going at it and I don't mean fighting. Right there on the rocks. One on top of the other. Now this would not seem to be that big of a deal until we discovered they were both men. Noticing us, they decided to stop. One saw my camera and wanted his photo taken. A nude photo. It's fun to take unusual photos to enhance my slide show but this was a bit too much.

Time to move on. After the waterfall and a Buddha image, we drove to the town of Lomas Beach. A clutter of stores from bars to travel agencies and rooms to rent. Almost like Khao San Road in Bangkok. We did book our next day's travel from the island. Our plan was to catch the morning 7:15 ferry to Surat Thani to get to the Malaysian border of Sungai Kolar. We would arrive at 5:30 PM. Cost would be $17.

Back at the cabin, I showered while Nancy took the bike and headed off to see a giant Buddha. I then sat on the deck and took it all in. Sitting on the deck, planning and just enjoying where I was. Coconuts were falling from the trees. The only thing you have to worry about here is that you don't get klonked on the head.

For dinner, I had the best chicken salad sandwich ever. Chit-chatted with our new friends. Then the hard part. Having to say good bye. Good luck. Happy trails.

Our ninth day out started by waking up at five in the morning to catch the six in the morning taxi to get to Naton Pier for the seven-fifteen express ferry. Here was a boat full of travelers. An English couple worried as they only had one more month to travel. Another, just starting his second year. All I know is where I'm headed for tonight. Tomorrow is still uncertain. Seems that way for others on the boat. All the Lonely Planet guidebooks are out.

On the mainland, we hopped on a 10-seater mini-van for what turned out to be a seven hour ride to Hat Yai. Van broke down on the way. Smoke started bellowing inside. We all climbed out rather quickly. We didn't know if we were going to get stuck in Hat Yai or continue on to Sungai Kolok. Another mini-van came for the last four-hour leg of the journey.

Originally, we were to get to the border at 5:30. I was hoping to cross over and spend the night in Kota Bahru. Since the border closes at six, it looks like we'll need to find a place in the not-so-happening town of Sungai Kolak. We met a fellow traveler. Mark, from Japan, joined us in our quest for the night's lodging. He welcomed the invitation. Upon arriving at the border, we found it opened. The three of us crossed and caught a cab to Kota Bharu. Out came the Lonely Planet guide for a place to stay. Decided on the Hotel Tokyo. The book said Rm 35 but the desk clerk said Rm 55 which was $9 per person. Raining and eleven at night, we didn't have much choice. What a pit. Very warm even with the fan. However, it had a flush toilet and toilet paper. We headed for the night market. Food stalls all around. I had a Murtabak. I'm feeling good. The others are having stomach problems.

The next morning we found the tourist center to make arrangements for the jungle train and the trip to Taman Negara Park. We also found a better place to stay. It was cleaner, had central air and only Rm 42 or $20. We had looked at a guest house that the tourist information guy had suggested. It turned out to be just a dorm room with a bath down the hall. Didn't know the price, nor did I care.

Said good-bye to our one day Japanese friend. Today will be a down day. When traveling with an adventure travel outfit, all days are planned. You are kept busy. Traveling on your own, you have down days. Down days consist of making plans, arrangements and such. Nothing too exciting here in Kota Bharu. We will be in bed early as a taxi will pick us up at five-thirty in the morning to take us to the six-thirty train.

It's Wednesday morning, September 4, at four-thirty. The hot shower felt good. Fahima, from the tourist office, doubled as our taxi driver. I knew I was overpaying for the cab ride at Rm 15. The eight hour train ride was only Rm 12. However, I wasn't going to look for a Rm 1 cost of a bus ride at this hour. Only a couple other backpackers. Otherwise, its the locals with all their packages. It's an old pit of a train. There are chickens clucking behind me. Rolled cigarette smoker across from me that smells like burning hay. Ten long hours on this train. It's a local train so it makes plenty of stops.

Made it to Jerantut. Met by a tour operator who took us to a hotel. That evening they explained about the National park. They seem to have a monopoly on this deal as they sweep backpackers from the train and plant them at their places. It is convenient and no extra cost.

At Taman Negara National Park, we stayed in a "chalet" on the "other side of the tracks". There is a lodge here that caters to the well-to-do. Rooms go for Rm 550 or $200. Plus there is a fancy restaurant. So much for a total jungle experience. Our room cost Rm 30 or $12.

We went on a 2 km hike up to a view point. Very hard going as it was straight up. Another hike took us to a canopy walkway. It is very hot here with very little breeze. I know I'm losing weight.

The next day's hike is what I was looking forward to doing. We were going to hike to a salt-lick overlook to spend the night in hopes of seeing wild life. It turned into a difficult trek.

The hike started off hard. We had to climb a steep hill with many tree roots to navigate over. Slippery mud once we made it to the top. Then slippery muddy path down. We traveled 3.2 km or about 2 miles in two hours. We finally made it to the hide. A hide is a hut on stilts to spend the night in hopes of spotting animals. The hut has eight bunks. Joining us in the hide are three Swiss and one from Poland. Trouble was, we could not converse with each other. Interesting set-up. Just a faucet for the flushing of the squat toilet and a lookout window with a bench for viewing. Doubt if we'll see anything but the sounds of the jungle is like music to my ears.

Here I am, in another jungle. Sweating, struggling to get here, wet, miserable and yet I still do it. Went to sleep at eight when it got dark.

Nothing else to do. Dozed on and off most of the night. Warm and uncomfortable. Up at 7:30. Did my bodily functions which I was so glad about. My health was still good.

At the hide we spotted a deer. That was it for the wildlife except for some centipedes and leeches that got on my feet. The clothes I slipped on were wet. Too humid to dry out. We hiked back from the jungle to the main area which consisted of fancy lodges. These lodges were used for the upper class tourists. The Japanese tourists were looking at Nancy and I like we were death warmed over. After a warm shower and cleaning my boots, I felt like a million bucks. I ate a banana pancake for lunch. Then we caught a launch back to Jerantut to spend the night.

Finally a meal. Six of us went to dinner and ordered up a feast. Vegetables, cashew chicken, sweet and sour pork, wild boar, rice and noodles. Everything was delicious. I hadn't eaten this good in two weeks. Washed it all down with a beer. All this cost me Rm 14 or $5.50. After dinner, we all headed to the night market. However, something was happening to me and I left the group running back to the hotel. I was going to explode and explode I did. After I recovered, I rejoined the group. That night, we stayed in a dorm room for $3.50. It came with a bed, fan and ants. Common bath and shower down the hall.

Sunday morning hustling about to catch the 10:30 am express train to Kuala Lumpur. It didn't matter. Train was sold out. No problem. We'll go to Temerloh and transfer. This turned out to be fun as there was a great Sunday market in Temerloh. I bought myself a wall hanging. From Temerloh, we caught the 1pm express bus to Kuala Lumpur (KL). We did not know what to expect when we got there. We'll just play it by ear. It didn't go well. We took the advice of the Lonely Planet guide. The guide gave a recommendation for the KL City Hotel. After walking for blocks trying to find this hotel, we found it. The location was convenient to areas of the city I wanted to be in. That's all this place offered. What a dump. I've stayed in dumps before but this place was the pits. Even the $15 was too much. The walls were cardboard, no windows. Bathroom down the hall. They didn't even leave the light on for you. The switch for the room was out in the hallway. There was one air conditioning unit for two rooms. An A/C unit was placed on a shelf in an opening to service two rooms. I was afraid to lay on the bed so out came my bedsheet. I knew where I was going to stay the next night. The Railway Hotel, where I had stayed six years before.

I walked around KL. It's a very nice city. I visited an Indian temple, then headed to Chinatown with a great outdoor market. Pirated tapes, CD's, shirt logos, VCR movies-a lot of fun. Everything is inexpensive.

What a pit this City Hotel. I needed a shower after the shower I took. The place was creepy, crawly. I left for the comforts of the Railway Hotel. So it was $55. I treated myself. Nancy was too cheap to spend one night in a nice place. She wanted to stay in a dorm. Fine with me. I went my own way. I told her I would see her on the train. The express train to Singapore leaves at 7:30am and costs $14. I would be right there as this is where the hotel was. Enjoyed a cold Anchor beer during happy hour. It was nice to feel fresh and clean again.

I had a good night of cheap shopping again. I saw a sad sight. A boy who was no more than seven years old, fast asleep on the sidewalk with a little cup out hoping for loose change.

Finally, a good night's sleep. Best I've had in two and a half weeks. The alarm had to wake me up.

Nancy was there at the train. We were in for a nice six hour train ride to Singapore. No trouble crossing the border. You do see a dog sniffing everything that comes by. It's on the lookout for drugs.

Upon arriving in Singapore, we called the YMCA. Singapore can be expensive. The Y's are the best for the least. It is a small room, but had central air, television, hot shower and flush toilet. We were in heaven. You couldn't ask for any more. We are in the final days of the adventure. Three days of shopping and sight-seeing in Singapore. Nothing too exciting. To me, Singapore is a city that works. Some may say it's too strict with all their rules but it is safe to walk the streets. The city is clean and efficient.

Getting around on the subway (MRT) or bus is a breeze. The only thing now is to catch the 6:30am flight for home.

Since we would have to be at the airport by 5am, we decided against staying at the hotel and instead opted to stay at the airport. We heard that the Changi airport was highly rated. We got to the airport around 9pm. Looking forward to the restaurants, shopping and whatever turned into a disappointment. Since we could not check in, we couldn't get to where the restaurants and shopping were. We couldn't even get to the transient hotel where you could get a room for six hours. I found a chair to spend the night after a light snack in the airport cafe.

I didn't sleep that night. Checked in at 4:30 am. No problems. No problems the rest of the way. I got on the plane and snuggled into my seat with a pillow and blanket. Maybe I'll watch a movie.

Some people like to travel in groups. Others, like to travel solo and meet people along the way. Traveling solo will force you to meet others. Otherwise, solo travel can get lonely. In a different part of the world, all alone may not be to fun. I've always enjoyed traveling with an adventure travel outfit but this time I wanted to try doing it with just a companion. The snag I ran into is the other. Who could I get to travel this kind of travel with me? I have a lot of friends but they would rather watch paint dry than to do the kind of trips I do. I didn't want to advertise and go with someone I didn't know. Unfortunately, Nancy turned out to be a disappointing travel companion. I still enjoyed the trip immensely but wish someone else had come along. Nancy was not fun.

So who do you travel with? How do you know if your travel partner will want to do the same things as you do? I don't think there is a sure answer. As I found out when I traveled with a group to Costa Rica, the trip was not all I wanted and I left the group. Nancy and I split up at times. Understand what each wants out of the trip. Be flexible enough to share in the other's likes or else split up and meet later to continue the adventure.

CHAPTER 11

▼

GUATEMALA: INDEPENDENT YET PLANNED

A kid I was a mentor to came over with his friend, Joe, as I was researching another possible adventure.

"What are you looking up?" Ben asked.

"I'm getting information about river rafting in Guatemala," I replied.

"Could I go?" Joe inquired.

I had known Joe for the six years I knew Ben. The two were childhood friends and I had taken both boys camping some years back so I knew Joe somewhat. I also knew that Joe had been in trouble with the law, had been kicked out of high school at the end of his senior year having to finish at an alternative school, and dabbled in drugs. Joe was not a bad kid, just wrong priorities. He dressed in black and had a pierced lip.

I hadn't even thought about who I might travel with. I asked Joe why he would want to travel with me. His reply was that he knew I did these type of trips and trusted my guidance to do something he would be otherwise unable to do. Not wanting to give Joe an outright no for an answer, I said that sure he could join me if he had a thousand bucks. That was my early estimate of what the cost to fly to Guatemala and the five day river rafting trip I was looking at. Thinking that a nineteen year old pizza delivery person who dressed like Bela Lugosi couldn't come up with the money, I looked for an easy way to discourage him. Well, bite me in the neck if he didn't surprise the hell out of me. Five hundred one week, four hundred the next week and then the final hundred and I still didn't have firm plans yet.

I always welcome a traveling companion. Would Joe and I get along? First off, I had to meet with Joe alone to discuss my type of traveling and what he wanted to get out of a trip such as I was planning. I told him in no uncertain terms would drugs of any kind be tolerated. I told him to rent the movie, *Midnight Express,* to see what happens getting caught with drugs in a foreign country. Also, I would recommend a dress code to blend in, not dress like a spook. In other words, generic T-shirts rather than ones with skulls and cross bones. Doing preliminary research, I found that Guatemala was not the safest country. Thieves targeted tourists as a source of income. I didn't need the problem of nagging Joe in how to appear and dress while traveling in a foreign country. All in all, I wondered if Joe would really go and want to be with an old fart like me. Nevertheless, I started doing my research. What did I want to see, how would I travel, when would I go? Unlike my other recent adventures that I planned where I would use local transportation and get around as needed, I was concerned about Guatemala. I would want this trip planned with knowing where I would spend each night and how I would get around. It would not be wherever I ended up is where I would be spending the night.

In the world of independent travel, there are firms that will do just that. Rather than traveling with an adventure travel outfit with a number of people, these firms will map out an itinerary for the independent traveler. You decide what you want to see and do and they will map out where you will stay, how you will get around, and advise you on other ideas to enjoy your own independent travel. One such firm, *California Native*, does just this. They arrange the transportation, lodging and guides. This is all well and good if you don't have the knowledge, time or confidence to plan your own trip. Naturally, there is a cost for their service. Since I like to do my own planning and research, I opted for me to be the travel planner. Make no mistake. Firms that do itinerary planning for the independent traveler can be a good source for a reliable adventure in a foreign or domestic location. Use them if you want a planned trip, yet independent, and you don't have the time to do your own planning.

With the advent of the computer age and all the information that's out there, I started in. My first stop is the library to research the travel guides to learn what there is to see and do. Could I make a varied activity adventure in Guatemala? The answer was yes. The focus would be a five-day white water river rafting trip on the Rio Cabon River which was rated class III and IV. Also included on my adventure would be a visit to the colonial town of Antigua, a hike up the active Pacaya volcano, and a flight to Flores to see the Mayan ruins in Tikal.

I estimated the trip to be twelve days. I would be able to go the second week in April, My research brought me to Mayan Expeditions for the river rafting portion. They had a US representative, Ken Johnson of Guatemala Unlimited. Through phone calls and E-mails, the rafting part of the trip was planned. I would be picked up at the hotel I stayed at on the day of departure.

The rest of the trip was planned through Voyageur Travel Service in Antigua. Through a couple of contacts, I got in touch with Sidija at Voyageur Travel. I had no knowledge of her previously but by the end, I made a good contact. When the many E-mails, bank wire, and decisions were done, my trip was planned just as if I had paid a firm such as California Native to do the planning. Voyageur Travel was a travel service who made a commission on the hotel rooms. The rates Sidija quoted were equal to what the guidebooks said. My trip was planned. All my hotel rooms were reserved and my transportation was arranged. Each day I knew what I would be doing and what rides I was to meet.

As the departure date kept nearing, I wondered if Joe would be going along. He paid me one thousand dollars, which was non-refundable. Through my terrific travel agent, Terry Kreisel, I was able to get a consolidator air fare to Guatemala City. The price was hundreds of dollars cheaper than what I could find on the net. Joe did get in trouble with the law but this did not interfere with his travel plans. Joe's mother brought him some "normal" clothes. I gave Joe my last pep talk and we were on our way.

It was a bright and beautiful Sunday afternoon when Joe's parents drove us to the airport. I met Joe's girlfriend who looked like Elvira. The two of them made a good looking couple-of spooks. We were to fly Continental Airlines to Houston and after a fifty minute layover, transfer to another Continental flight to Guatemala City. So what happens? As usual, something didn't gel. Just as we were checking in for our flight out of Minneapolis, another Continental agent was switching the departure time of our flight which would leave forty minutes later. This was not good. Right in front of our eyes we were seeing a problem arise. I asked the agent if we could switch over to a Northwest Airlines flight leaving at 2:30 rather than our original flight at 3:10. Even though we had a consolidator fare, being Continental and Northwest were in some kind of partnership, the switch was made. Good thing as we just barley made the connecting flight to Guatemala City. We would never have made it if we did the original flight schedule. Things went smoothly in Guatemala City. A young man helped us with a call to the hotel we would stay at to see if a car would come for us. When this didn't pan out, he got us a cab, told us how much it would cost and so away we went. The airport guest house had our name for the reservation. After checking in and dropping off our bags in the room, I did what I love to do. I struck up a conversation with a fellow adventurer in the lobby area. Amy was a twenty-eight year old former IT person who worked eighty hours a week and no time off as it *wasn't convenient.*

Her vacations were two weeks pay. In other words, she never was able to take time off. She just got paid. She left behind the rat race and a $60,000 salary to get certified as a dive master on an island off Honduras. She relied on tips for any pay. To supplement her new passion for diving, she worked as a waitress, bartender and movie usher. Barely making a living, she has never been happier. She is here in Guatemala to meet a friend and see some of the country.

Joe and I head for bed close to midnight. The room is basic with a fan to cool the room and a shower that doesn't work. Rising at seven and after a breakfast of corn flakes and toast, we get picked up for the ride to Antigua. We're dropped off at Hotel Posada San Pedro. Basic room for $25 that includes two beds and private bath. After getting situated, we headed out to walk the city. Antigua is easy to get around and for that reason there is no local transportation as everything is in walking distance. Antigua is an old colonial style town with cobblestone streets. We walk the open and covered street market on the west end of town and then head to the Central Park to do some people watching. As we are sitting on a bench, we are ambushed by vendors. We then pop into a couple of local churches to see what they have to offer in way of charm. They didn't. They were nothing special so we headed back to the hotel where we took a nap. After waking and cleaning up, we used the guide book to find a place for dinner. After a great pasta dinner, we hit a local bar for a couple of cervesas. Not much else was going on so we headed back to the hotel and after a couple of games of 500, we called it a day and hit the sack.

We slept in until nine which was probably going to be our last good sleep for a while. I had a great cheese omelet for breakfast, than headed to Voyageur Travel Agency to meet up with Sidija to settle up my account. We waited around until one, then caught our ride to the Pacaya Volcano for our trek.

The ride up was an adventure. The driver of the mini-van had to stop about three times to fill the radiator with water as the ride was an uphill struggle. There were about fifteen people going on this trek with Joe and

I, the only Americans. As the driver was trying to go around a guy riding his bike on the side of the road, a truck was approaching from the opposite direction. Our driver cut back into the lane and we heard a thud. We all looked out the back as the driver kept going to notice the guy on the bike had been knocked over. Now in my country, this is called hit and run with a sidebar called lawsuit. We tried to tell the driver, but he kept on going. We again looked back and saw the guy dust himself off and get back on the bike to continue his journey.

Reaching the turnoff to start up the mountain was just a dirt and gravel road which was very slow going. Having to stop to fill the radiator, I thought we would never get to the starting point. However, once there, the guide started his speech about the climb. Only one problem. He only spoke Spanish so I asked a Belgium guy to interpret for me. How come all the Europeans know all the languages? I've been struggling with learning Spanish for years. I found out this trek up over 10,000 ft. was not going to be easy for me. The route was straight up. We were accompanied by a gun toting security guard as tourists are robbed as they climb the popular treks. I can see it now. A gun fight and I'm in the middle. What was worst was that I was trailing the rest of the group in the climb and even the guard couldn't stay with me. However, with the breaks, I was able to keep up and staggered to catch up to the group before the final assent. This final assent was not going to be easy. Hell, I'm getting to old for this shit. The reason for the difficulty, was that we were climbing on fine ground loose lava rock. For every three steps forward, you slid two steps back. A smile came across my face. I'm about to pass a couple. I won't be the last one up. Near the top, I can feel the sulfur burning my eyes and the smoke coming up from the hot rocks I was walking on. At the top, it was a sight to behold. Looking down into the crater is a bubbly pool of flaming rock. The heat and poison gases are hard to take and I have to turn away. Someone takes a picture of Joe and I which later turned out to look like two guys looking like death warmed over. We were both exhausted, dripping with sweat and dirty. However, a euphoria comes over me. I feel a real sense of accomplishment. A real achievement. I wish I had worked myself up into better condition before the trip so this hike wouldn't have been as difficult. Now it was time to turn around and head down. This turned out to be a lot of fun. With the fine grain of the rock along with the steep slant of the mountain, we were actually running down the mountain but being held up by the fine ground lava. It was like skiing down a mountain without skis. Down at the bottom of the mountain, we had some drinks and headed back. The security guard rode along the long dirt rode until we reached the main road. It was now dark and rainy as we were heading home. However, the piece of crap mini-bus didn't have any windshield wipers. Just the hands and rag of the driver. I buckled my seat belt.

Finally back, Joe and I are starved, so we head for a restaurant for dinner. No later than two minutes after we order, the power on the street and in the restaurant goes out. Luckily, they can still make our dinner. I didn't want to know how and having a candlelight dinner with Joe sitting across from me was not my idea of a nice cozy dinner. We got back to the hotel about eleven and had a big decision to make. A shuttle service would be picking us up at four thirty the next morning to get us to the airport to catch our flight to Flores. Do we sleep three to four hours or do we stay up all night? Being exhausted from the volcano trek, I know if I cuddle up for bed, I won't wake up anytime soon. A plan was devised over a game of 500 rummy. We kept the lights on in the room and I kept my glasses on and did not get under the covers. I set the alarm and just dozed. This worked well. By the time three thirty rolled around, I wasn't in a slumber and was able to wake easily. I got Joe up and we were ready to meet the remarkable on-time van that was picking us up at four thirty.

We were taking Tikal Airlines from Guatemala City to Flores which was less than an hour flight. If you have the craving to hijack a plane, this would be an easy one to do. There is no security check. We had to go outside to get on the plane which any person could have come on from the ground area. In fact, we had to cross a regular street to get to the tarmac and onto the plane.

At the airport, I make arrangements for a ride to the hotel to check in and drop off our luggage. From here we were taken to the Mayan ruins of Tikal where awesome sights of the ruins are reached by walking the paths. They are a magnificent sight to see. However, Joe and I were wiped. Having done the volcano climb the night before and getting no sleep, we did not have the energy or will to climb the steps of the Mayan ruins. We lazily walked around some more until our ride back to the hotel came. We did not want to lay down as we knew we would not wake up and it was only three in the afternoon. The Hotel Peten, where we were staying, was on the lake and had a balcony overlooking the lake along with having an indoor swimming pool, air conditioning, restaurant and bar all for forty dollars. So we head for the pool and get a couple of beers to discuss what we should do the next day. About the only thing in the area to do that might be of interest was a four-hour jungle trek. This thought in the tired state we were in sounded horrible, yet we did not want to hang in the town of Flores all day. Then a light bulb clicked on in my head. An idea that may be bizarre but was worth seeing if it could be done. The idea was to go to Belize for the day and go snorkeling. My guide book said that plane fare would be about $80 round trip. However, when we checked with two different travel agencies, we found that the price was $192 each. So what about a bus? I checked with the hotel travel service and they had me catching a five in the morning bus coming back at three in the after-noon. The bus ride would be four hours. Cost was $40 round trip. This would not give us enough time in Belize. It was now 5pm and time was running out in making plans for the next day. I found a very helpful travel agent, mainly because we could understand each other with my little Spanish and her little English. We arranged to take the five in the morning bus, getting to Belize City at nine, then catch the same bus as it returns to Belize City at five in the afternoon. This sounded great. We would have the whole day in Belize. This sounded a whole lot better than being in

Flores so I paid with my credit card $80 for the both of us and our plans were made. Once again, we would have to get up early but we were in a deep sleep by nine.

Sure enough. At five the next morning, the mini-bus was there. It would be a four hour-ride to Belize City. Crossing the border was no problem. Exit tax of ten Quetzales or about $1.30. This was not a tourist bus but a regular scheduled bus. However, the driver knew that we, the two gringo's, would be coming back with him. So when we reached Belize City, the bus driver stopped the bus, got out and came to talk to me from the window. He asked me if I comprende Espanol? Do I understand Spanish. I answered muy poco-very little. This did not stop him from going into a long and fast speech in Spanish about how he would pick us up at this spot at five, but that he was dropping us off at the boat docks as that was the normal stop to drop off passengers. However, he would be going up the coast and coming by this spot at five to pick us up. So be here at this spot. Naturally, I only picked up a few words so when I turned my head in a-what did he say look-someone told me the plan. So once we got this figured out and dropped off at the boat docks, it was time to find out about snorkeling. The boat docks are where open launches take passengers to the cays or islands.

A shady looking guy standing outside the ticket cage asked if he could help us. I saw him helping with loading passengers on the 9am launch so I figured he worked there. However, with him just standing around and asking if he could help me, I thought of Jack Lemmon and Sandy Dennis in the *Out of Towners* where a man approaches them in a hotel and says he knows of a room they can get for the night. Being desperate for a room, Jack and Sandy follow this character for a block before he turns on them and robs them. I decided to trust this guy for now rather than waste time walking the city trying to find a travel agency or dive shop to set up a snorkeling trip. Time was not on my side. I told him what I wanted to do and was it possible with the short time we had? Not really, but after he made a couple of calls-out of sight of us-he said we could have our own launch to take us snorkeling and looking for manatees. The cost was high, as he frowned, saying the price was high at $100 each. I knew this was high. However, I looked at the situation. Everything we wanted to do, we could do now and not have to schlep around trying to find a cheaper price and lose valuable time and possibly having the day go bust. I had my emergency traveler checks with me that I first bought for one of my trips a zillion years ago. I never regarded this as money I had. So I put my trust in this guy who also was so kind as to show me where I could cash my traveler checks to get him the $200 in Belize money. I handed it over to my "new" friend. This was setting up to be a classic rip-off. He told us to be back in one hour and bring a lunch. He gave me a receipt from a receipt book. No company name or any identification of him or the company taking us snorkeling.

Joe and I went to have breakfast. We had about an hour to kill. While having breakfast we looked at the receipt. We laughed but I was thinking if I do get ripped off, it's all my fault. I knew better, to be more cautious. Upon finishing breakfast and getting a packed sandwich, we headed back to the docks. Would this guy be there? Was I out $200? Well, blow me down, was I surprised when I saw him. This was a good sign. He was collecting tickets and helping people on the launch to Cay Caulker, a major island for water sports. Joe and I sat waiting for a sign that it was our turn to leave. At ten-forty, Tyrone said our launch was here along with the boat man. Have a good time.

So that is what we did. It was a beautiful, sunny day as we boated a half hour to beautiful Geoff's Cay. A cay no larger than a football field to snorkel and lay on the beach. I was in awe that everything we wanted to do came together. The last minute bus ride, the chance of finding a snorkeling trip to match the little time we had to work with. Yes, I paid twice as much as I needed to but that's the breaks. To me it was worth it and that's all that mattered. The warm Caribbean water was perfectly clear and the snorkeling was good. Relaxing on the beach, resting my weary body and catching rays. I was smiling. Joe was having the time of his life. He had never done this before. The alternative could have been walking around Belize City which would have been a bore or hiking a jungle trail in Flores which would have been hot and hotter. Here we were, taken to two snorkeling areas to enjoy the water and the sun. The sun. Two weeks previous to this trip, I was at my time share in Aruba and got toasted on a day of sailing and snorkeling. My peeling skin was getting back to normal. I left the sun lotion in the room back at the hotel. After snorkeling, Carlos, took us to a protected area to observe manatees. He would pole the launch around in hopes of spotting the endangered sea cows. We did spot some as they came to the surface for air. This was fun and after, we headed back to the boat docks reaching them at four. We had an hour to catch the bus. There was Tyrone who asked us how we liked the outing. I shook his hand and said thanks. Then we went looking for that bus stop. I bought a newspaper to learn that crime in Belize is like anywhere else in the world. Thievery and killing with the killers getting the death penalty for their crime. We ate our forgotten lunch at the bus stop and sure enough, even ten minutes early, the mini-bus comes by and picks us up. It was the same driver. A long day for him. Leave Flores at five in the morning, returning to Flores at eight in the evening.

My experience in leaving and entering countries is that upon leaving a country, an exit tax is sometimes collected. When we left Guatemala this morning, we paid ten Quetzals each or about $1.30. Now crossing the border, leaving Belize and coming back into Guatemala, we were not charged any exit tax in Belize. However, going through immigration to get into Guatemala, the official wanted $10 apiece. I thought this was a little strange. Not to fall for the uninformed tourist trap, I questioned the official. I told him that I paid this morning an exit tax. Why is this entry tax being charged? He gave me some bullshit story of having to pay double when I left Guatemala airport if I didn't pay this portion now. I told him this is not right. You don't pay to enter a country. Then a couple of Americans from Idaho, who were going to school in Mazatlan and were enjoying spring break, got into the fracas. They spoke Spanish and questioned this tax in a language the official could better understand. They got the same reply. If we didn't pay now, we would pay double later and he would put a star by our names so this would happen. We all said we would pay it later when we left the country. Finally, we got our passports stamped along with a star by our names in his ledger and got back on the bus to Flores. Driving back, the girl asked the driver about the tax issue. He said there is no tax and that these border officials try their underhanded ways on weary, uninformed tourists. I felt good that I challenged this and did not back down. It is just the norm that as a traveler in a foreign country, there are more times than not when you end up spending more than you should for a cab, tax, and so on. It just happens. So when you win one, you smile and pat yourself on the back. It's one for the good guys.

Back at the hotel, Joe and I look each other over to see how badly sunburned we were. I felt a nice glow and was richly tanned. Joe was hurting. He was a french fry.

The next day, Friday, would be a down day. Being that we were not flying back to Guatemala City until four, I slept late, to about nine. Then I enjoyed one of my pleasures of traveling by sitting in a foreign country, enjoying the scenery which was on the patio overlooking the lake, having a cup of coffee and writing. Life is good. I take it all in, realizing where I am and doing what I love. Yes, life is good today.

To pass the time until it was time to leave, we went shopping, had a lousy lunch, and played cards. Sitting next to me on the plane was a family from Seattle. They were traveling with their two young children of five and seven. I asked them if they missed the turn to Disney World. They said their friends couldn't understand why they would vacation in Guatemala. The kids were immensely enjoying themselves and this trip would be a lot more memorable than visiting the mouse and his friends. I asked if they did adventures before they had kids. They replied, not really. It was just something they wanted to do.

We got back to the Continental Ritz Hotel and even though they didn't have the reservation we made before we left, we were able to get a room. Joe is hurting badly from his sunburn. We packed for the rafting trip and went to bed. I must have been tired as the alarm woke me up the next morning. Usually, I wake up before the alarm.

Waiting in the lobby for our rafting company to pick us up, the phone rang which was for me. It was the rafting company saying they would be late. Upon being picked up, I learned that Joe and I would be the only outsiders on the trip. The others were our guides, a trainee, and a girl from Finland who was studying travel and working freelance for Mayan Expeditions to promote the rafting at hotels and travel agencies. We get a more personalized trip but we won't have the camaraderie of fellow travelers.

The first day was a travel day with a stop at the Natural Reserve Biotopo Mario Dari. The road up the mountain was a single lane dirt road. When two vehicles would meet, a maneuvering would take place to avoid any one vehicle going over the edge. Joe and I were wondering what this hotel would be like being out in nowhere land. We came upon a sort of oasis. Nice hotel area of trees, pools-not for swimming-rooms and sounds of the jungle. Joe and I drank a few cervesas and discussed world problems or whatever two beer drinking travelers talk about. Hit the sack about ten only to get woken up by a loud cock-a-doodle-do at five in the morning. The walls are thin and noises abound. I shared a cold dripping shower with a couple of spiders and crickets.

We started off the morning walking and climbing Crutus Lanking Caves. The paths would not be United States certified. Slippery rocks, ladders, boldering is the only way to explore this wonderful sight. From here, we met our river rafting guides, gathered gear and headed for the river. The weather is hot and clear. It was nice to be on the water. However, the water level was very low and river rafting can be different from one day to the next depending on the water level. As we were doing the float, our guide, Eric, a twenty three year old Californian river guide, said to sit in the raft. I had never been told in all my rafting trips to sit in the raft.

Usually you're out paddling and working your way through the rapids. After going through this particular rapid, I saw why we had to sit in the raft. If I was out on the edge paddling like normally I would, I would have ended up swimming.

We camped along the shore with the sights and sounds of the jungle. A pasta dinner with chicken and sauce was on the menu. Then a relaxing moment of having a cup of coffee while taking in the sights, sounds, and situation of the moment. It was very nice.

Woke at the crack of dawn due to-what else, a rooster. The day was long. Due to the low water level, there was a lot more paddling than rapids to enjoy. In the afternoon, we stopped for lunch and picked up eight rafters who were just doing a day trip. That night we set up camp in some field along with the locals, cows and pigs. Once again, Mr. Rooster let me know when the day was beginning. The rafting started off fun going through some class IV rapids. If the water level was higher, this would have been some ride. After the water calmed down, we had an exciting side trip. Gathering flashlights, we explored an amazing cave. Nothing like any cave exploring I've ever done. Pitch black with just the beam of our lights, we made our way through waist high deep waters, up rock ledges only to jump in a pool of water trying to hold our flashlights above our heads to keep them out of the water. Like a science fiction scene where something grabs one of us and pulls us under. Continuing our exploration, we hit a section with bats flying all around us. We shut off the flashlights and listened to the fluttering of the bats as we were in complete darkness. Javier, the trainee guide, was not enjoying any of this. Joe and I thought it was awesome. After swimming and climbing our way out of the cave, it was back on the rafts only to find a section of paradise at the next stop. Pools of hot mineral springs covered by the trees of the jungle. You melt away with total relaxation as you sit in your own private pool, hear nothing but the sounds of the mini waterfalls falling on either side of your head. If this is heaven, than Lord, take me now. Joe, who had never known total drug free bliss, was awed by the soothing, relaxing pool of hot mineral water as he soaked it all in. Even though lunch was being served, who could move?

Back on the river again and from the mineral springs to the end, the water was slow and the paddling was much. We jumped out at times to swim and push the raft along. Finally, the end of the rafting trip. A bus came to pick us up and it was time to say good-by to our rafting guides, Ariel and Eric. They would need to get ready for another group tomorrow. Javiar and the Finnish girl accompanied us to the noisy, nothing town of El Estor. The Hotel Marisabela was nothing special but had two beds, hot shower, and a fan. Javiar and the girl joined us for dinner which afterward, I said good-by to Joe and Javiar so they could go out to where the music was blaring and have a good time. Me being the old man, well, it was time for bed but there is enough noise of the blaring music and barking dogs to keep me up all night. Joe had come back and gone to sleep but the music kept going and going until two in the morning. I was thirsty and wide awake listening to the blaring music coming from who knows where. Ricky Martin singing, Uno, Dos, Tres. I was pissed, so I borrowed a soda pop from the cooler. I may forget to pay. The roosters and workmen were up bright and early so guess what? So was I! There was no dark shade for the room, just a flimsy curtain. It's 6am, I'm wide awake with nothing to do as Javiar is not going to get us for breakfast for another two hours.

The day was basically a traveling day back to Guatemala City with uninteresting stops at Finca Pariso, a hot springs that I didn't go into, Castillo de San Felipe, a fort that was closed due to an earthquake the previous year, and the ruins of Quirgua, which were not much. We said good-by to Synnone, the Finnish girl, during lunch as she was continuing on in another direction. Back at the Ritz Continental in Guatemala City, we said good-by to Romero and Javiar. Grabbed a steak sandwich for dinner, then once around the block and into bed. No roosters to wake me but the traffic noise is like I'm sleeping on the street.

Our final full day, we slept in the best we could. Upon awaking, cleaning up and having breakfast in which I had panqueques, we headed to the central market. There was a mass of people due to a parade celebrating Easter. We could barely move but found the central market which was all underground. We walked the shops and even bought a couple of things. After getting back to the hotel and checking out, we headed to zone 13, the swanky part of town to stay at the Holiday Inn. I stay at a nice hotel the final night of any adventure trip to work my way back to civilization. As we walked the streets, the stores were closed due to Sementa week. We did find a broken down mini-golf course open which we got involved in with the loser buying the winner a beer. Then my final dinner ritual of a nice restaurant and a good meal. We found just that at an outside restaurant and a grand meal of a filet steak, potato and glass of wine followed by a cup of coffee. We rekindled memories of the trip, how much fun we had and how we enjoyed each other's company. I enjoyed taking Joe as I had seen the look of awe and wonderment on all the new experiences he had. This was a treat for me as well as him.

Finally, we had a good night's sleep and caught the shuttle to the airport in the morning. The adventure after the adventure never came but we were delayed two hours in Houston. While others were calling home to say they would be late, I was calling my hairdresser, as the sun from the trip bleached my hair and the gray was showing. After all, I had to be to work on Tuesday.

CHAPTER 12

▼

ARUBA: TIME SHARE ADVENTURES

Let's face it. Not all adventure trips for the working stiff have to involve stress, strain, camping, hiking, or high adventure. Not all shapes and sizes of people can do some adventures. A lot of working stiffs just want to get away and relax. Lay around with no cares. I found a way to have an adventure in a more easier and relaxed fashion. I became involved in a time share.

I used to conduct seminars for a time-share operator for a resort in the Northern Lakes area of Minnesota. People were invited to a free dinner where they would hear about owning a piece of a resort. With a time-share, you purchase and own one unit, one week out of each year. The same week at the same resort year after year. My job was to get the people committed to visit the resort. To entice them further, they would be eligible to win a prize after touring the resort. I would get $100 for every couple that went up. It was a beautiful resort, but I thought who would want to go to the same place year after year. I found out years later that owning a time-share can be a new way to find adventure at a leisurely pace.

I am blessed with wonderful friends. Different friends have different styles in which they live. John and Linda like the restful places to go. If they have a casino and good shopping that's the place for them. They had purchased a time-share in Aruba, a tiny tourist island twenty miles off the coast of Venezuela. One year they invited me to be their guest. This sounded great. A chance to be in a foreign country. A chance to feel how the "rich and famous" travel.

I didn't have to have shots. I didn't have to get in shape. I didn't need visas. This was to easy and yet an adventure at the same time.

Travel day came and no problems. We took a plane to Miami where we transferred to Air Aruba. I didn't have frequent flyer tickets for this trip. We arrived in Aruba. It was hot. The resort was nice. Beautiful pool area with swim up bar overlooking the ocean. All we had to do was know when to roll over so we would not sun burn. Explored the island in the afternoon. Had a great dinner at night and tried our luck in the casinos. I am not a big time gambler but enjoy the casinos. I was not doing well.

John and Linda had come to Aruba for an anniversary. They bought during construction and purchased two weeks. I really liked Aruba. I could see me coming here each year to get out of the Minnesota winter. Plus, by owning in Aruba, I would be able to join a network called Interval International. This would allow me to "bank" my week in exchange for another week anywhere in the world that was a member complex. What neat adventures I could plan for.

I decided to look into purchasing a unit. I told John and Linda that I would purchase the same week they had. This would mean we'd be friends for life. After they thought about this a while looking at each other and my telling them what they could do to themselves, we laughed.

John accompanied me up to the sales office where I would encounter Jose. The price was $7,200. 15% discount if I paid cash within 60 days by arranging my own financing and not going through them. Also, I would receive $250 in match play money for use in the resort's casino. I tried to negotiate but to no avail. This was the price. After an impasse, I was taken to the sales manager. Just like buying a car. Again, no negotiation. I told them thanks, that I would have to think about it. John and I left to go back to the room. I was leaning to making a purchase. I would arrange my own financing to which I would save 15%. That would save me about $1,100. Being able to exchange my week for any other week any where in the world sounded appealing. John knew I was slipping. Not five minutes later, a knock on the door. It was Jose. If I would purchase today, the price still would be $7,200 and a 15% discount for the balance to be paid in the 60 days. Plus, I would get a one-time bonus week-a free week to use at this resort or any other resort in the network, plus $450 in casino match play money. Since I was losing at the tables, I asked how soon I could get the match play money. Jose said right away. Hell, I would worry about the $7,200 later. Right now I wanted the $450 match play money. I signed the papers. John was laughing all the time. He knew I would purchase.

I made the right decision. I love Aruba. We have brought friends down. It's a great winter get-away. Unlike a hotel room where it's crowded, I have a regular apartment. My unit sleeps four, has a kitchen, living room and patio. We gather in each other's units, sit around and chat. We don't have the feeling that we have to go out to be together.

Now the best part to owning a time-share. What I consider the adventure of owning a time-share. Being able to see a different area, have a place to stay for only an exchange fee. John and Linda took my girlfriend and I to Lake Tahoe. We in turn, took them to Puerto Rico. For a graduation gift, I took my godson to a resort in Portugal. Another time my godson, Ben, and I went to a time-share in Singapore. I've also exchanged for a place in Norway. From these places, we plan mini-adventures. I'm now looking forward to going through the exchange catalog to see where to go next.

This type of adventuring is costly. The initial cost of purchasing, a yearly maintenance fee, plus an exchange fee if you trade. Not to mention the difficulty and loss should you want to sell your unit. However, owning a time-share does make you take a trip each year. You can have the resort try renting your week if you desire. Also the cost for a hotel room in Aruba runs $300 and up per day. I'm glad I purchased. If you're considering purchasing a time-share, know what you are getting. For instance, you cannot purchase an inexpensive week in Minnesota's winter time to be able to exchange for a winter get-away at a member resort in Hawaii. Costs for resorts are skyrocketing. Maintenance fees go up. Aside from all this, I have had great, professional service when I have exchanged. No hassles at all. I have found a great way to have an adventure and not risk my weary body. If I'm lucky while in Aruba to be able to get going by 9:30 in the morning, I can participate in water aerobics. Yeah, right.

CHAPTER 13

▼

LOCAL ADVENTURES: ADVENTURES IN YOUR OWN BACKYARD

Not all adventures have to involve going to exotic locations. The previous adventures I did were mostly as a single but a companion could have gone along. What if you have a family? Yes, you are a working stiff and want an adventure, but you also have a family to consider. When taking the family, try to stay away from the motel scene of television and video games. Depending where you live, take a 360 degree look around to see where you could go with just a day's drive ahead.

My first adventure with a family member was when my nephew, Mike, graduated high school. I asked what he would like for a graduation gift. I could give a typical gift like a tie or a piece of luggage. Or I could take you on an adventure trip. His eyes lit up. Out came a map of North America including Canada. We lived in Minnesota. Where could we go that would be reachable with a couple of days driving and be something new? Mike pointed north, north into Canada. We would be camping along the way, until the road came to an end in Thompson, Ontario. However, that didn't stop us. We decided to go to the Polar Bear capital of the world, Churchill. The only way to Churchill is an all night train. There are no roads. The trip turned out great. Mike was an excellent traveling companion. We learned about a different type of existence up in the tundra of Canada. It was the middle of July and we were freezing on an ice slick on Hudson Bay.

Planning an adventure always gave me a thrill. I was, for a short period in my life, a single parent. I wanted to take David and a couple of his friends on an adventure. Where could I go within a day's drive? How could I make the trip sound more exciting than just saying, we're going hiking up north?

That's when your imagination and planning comes in. The following is what I was able to do in my neck of the woods. Now, could you do something similar in your area?

June 23 -Travel to Tower Soudan State Park. Mine exploration at 2,400 feet below surface. Camp at Bear Head Lake State Park.

June 24 -Hike Angleworm Trail. Camp along trail by lake.

June 25 -Hike Angleworm Trail. Camp along trail by lake.

June 26 -Finish hike. Camp at Split Rock Lighthouse State Park.

June 27 -Whitewater rafting on St. Louis River. Travel back to Minneapolis.

The Angleworm Trail covers fourteen miles of remote wilderness in Superior National Forest. There will be high rock ridges to climb with scenic overlooks. Wildlife of moose, deer, bear, and wolves inhabit the area. Smaller mammals such as fox, red squirrels, beaver, weasel, otter and mink can add pleasure to the trip. Loons and Canada Jays are common. Sighting an eagle or osprey is possible.

Another year, I planned the following. You can plan a family adventure using the same technique. Get the family involved in the planning. It could be the most rewarding time you'll have.

A Western Adventure awaits from camping and spelunking in the Black Hills of South Dakota to fishing, hiking, exploring in the Big Horn Mountain Range in Wyoming.

June 24 -Drive to and camp in Badlands National Park.

June 25 -Visit Mt. Rushmore in morning. Afternoon hike up Harney Peak, the highest point in South Dakota (7,242 feet).

June 26 -Custer State Park-habitat of one of the world's largest free-roaming bison herds. Other large mammals living in the park include elk, big horn sheep, pronghorn antelope, mountain goats and deer. We'll drive the Needles Scenic Drive through the oddly shaped, weathered granite spires. Several hairpin curves and narrow tunnels.

Afternoon spelunking in Wind Cave. Got its name from the strong wind currents that blow alternately in and out of the cave.

Evening swim in the world's largest natural spring-fed warm water indoor pool at Evan's Plunge. Camp Sylvan Lake.

June 27-July 1-Drive to Bighorn Mountains. Camp, fish, explore areas like tie flume where railroad ties were cut on top of Bighorn Mountain and sent down to the prairie on wooden chutes. Dead Swede area named after a timberman that no one knew his name. Hike Black Mountain Lookout at 9,489 feet. Fish for rainbow trout at Twin Lakes.

July 2-4-Head home, camping along the way.

The Bighorn Mountains offer outstanding scenery-mountains, streams, lakes and forests. A variety of wildlife includes elk, deer, moose, bighorn sheep, black bear, and coyotes, as well as bald and golden eagles.

The Bighorn National Forest was established by President Grover Cleveland on February 22, 1897. This National Forest is about 80 miles long and 30 miles wide.

Be creative. Make it fun. Make a trip to Disney World an adventure. We'll journey on a wild ride with a toad, see far away places in the small, small world, ride through a haunted house with flying ghosts swooping down on you. The adventure planning takes an effort. Do it. The time and trouble will be worth it.

CHAPTER 14

▼

COPPER CANYON: GIVING THE GIFT OF ADVENTURE

At one time or another, giving a gift for a wedding, special birthday or graduation is something that will happen. When my nephew graduated high school, I asked him if he would like a typical gift of a piece of luggage, a tie, or an adventure trip. His eyes widened as the word "trip" spilled out of his mouth. Out came a map of North America and I said "Where to?" So it came, an adventure to the Polar Bear capital of the world, Churchill, Canada. We traveled by car and train for a most wonderful time. I had taken my godson to Portugal as a graduation gift. He was so excited afterward that he went to study in Italy for a year and travel Europe.

It is easy for me to do this being single. It gives me great joy to introduce my passion for adventure to someone. However, instead of a typical gift that will be forgotten or returned within a week, I suggest something more exciting. I recommend a pooling of friends to donate towards an adventure. Since cash seems to be the easiest gift, with the graduate's permission, contact an adventure travel outfit, donate to an adventure, and give the greatest gift, the greatest experience in the graduate's life. It will be a gift never forgotten and will last a lifetime.

Matt was an intern at the corporation I worked at. Our jobs interacted at times and casual conversations took place. Since he was a graduating senior and headed for college in the fall, I mentioned to him to get a friend and go on an adventure trip. I had been doing adventure trips for over 20 years and explained why he should do this before college and work started. This would probably be his last summer for a long time to take time for a trip.

We had lunch together and I showed him some adventure travel magazines, told him of some of my adventures and gave him ideas of what he could do and where he could go. I said, "If you want to try a foreign country and try out your Spanish, head to the Copper Canyon in Mexico." I said, "I've always wanted to go there."

Matt says, "Let's go!" I was stunned. Anytime I have a chance at an adventure and a willing companion, my travel juices start flowing.

I had a lot to talk over with Matt including finding out if we would be compatible travel companions. I was another generation older than Matt. However, after a couple of discussions, and yes, meeting his parents, a graduation gift of going to the Copper Canyon started to become a reality. I had a hard time believing this trip was going to happen.

Naturally, getting to the starting point is the biggest cost. The easiest would be to fly from Minneapolis to Chihuahua and catch the Chihuahua Al Pacifico, the train through the Copper Canyon, with jump off spots along the route. Cost $645. After looking at different ways including flying to El Paso, crossing the border into Mexico, hopping a bus to Chihuahua, we decided this lost day, even though $300 cheaper, was not worth it.

I learned Matt had never been on an airplane. Nor had he been out of the state. Now here he was going out of the country. It gives me a thrill that I can introduce and share my passion for adventure travel.

Departure day arrived. We were to fly to Phoenix to catch Aero Mexico to Chihuahua. Hopefully, Northwest Airlines would leave on time. They had been having labor disputes and flights were late or being canceled. However, we got off on time, had a three-hour layover in Phoenix, caught Aero Mexico to Hermosilla, went through customs, back on the plane to Chihuahua. No problemas whatsoever! Even getting from the airport to the hotel was slick. My Espanol was working well and I really am bad at the language. Matt wasn't as knowledgeable as I thought, Who cares! It's more fun this way.

Arriving at Hotel San Juan, I found out the reservation I thought I had, I really didn't. Or else they couldn't understand me. Anyway, we got a double room for 72 pesos, or $9. After getting situated, we headed out. We walked the downtown area with all vendors and stopped at some side cafe for tacos and enchiladas. A lot different then Taco Bell back home. Unfortunately, we got lost walking the streets but our little map got us back. Hit the sack at 9:30 as we had to get up at 4am to get to the train the next morning. Noisy hotel. Woke up three times. Up at four. A great hot shower. You appreciate these little things in life when you travel budget style. The taxi we ordered was there on time at 5am to drive us to the train which was just fifteen minutes away. Good thing we got there early. All the guidebooks said the train left at seven. We found out it was leaving at six. The schedule changed a month earlier.

We were hoping to have breakfast on the train. However, no coche a comer-no dining car. We are starving. It will be five hours until Creel, the first major stop. Luckily, the train stopped about 9:30 where we were able to get some juice and bland wafers. Next stop was Divisadero. There was a fifteen minute stop and what a stop. We saw the most magnificent site. We were in the Copper Canyon. What a grand canyon of a view here. We would plan to stay overnight on the way back. We were able to pick up some hot food from the vendors and get back on the train. We made it to Bahuichivo where we hoped to catch a bus. However, since this was not the tourist season, the hotel we were going to stay at had a car waiting hoping to grab some travelers. Three Frenchmen and a Mexican senora joined us. The road to the hotel was non-existent. The area is built on a rock. Everything is rocky and dusty. Rainy season starts in forty-five days. Very dry. Rivers are non-existent.

Strange hotel. Rooms cost $120. However, there is a dorm that Matt and I are staying in that cost $10. It's just as nice except it has bunk beds as it is a dormitory-style room. The others stayed in another dorm and Matt and I had this whole dorm to ourselves as the six of us were the only guests. Wonderful home made enchiladas for dinner, which cost us only $5. After dinner we all hiked up to what should have been a waterfall. Our guide, Jim, was an American from Northern Minnesota. It was nice to be out hiking after having ridden the train all day. Back at the hotel, we had some drinks and chatted among our new friends for a day. This is always one of the highlights of adventure travel for me. Meeting and learning from fellow travelers. It is a camaraderie that only budget travelers have. Three languages of Spanish, French and English are being spoken. After a long day, it was time for bed at ten.

Slept pretty good except for the barking dogs and the crowing rooster at the break of dawn. After breakfast, Matt and I said good-bye to the others. They were headed out and we were headed for a hike along the rim of the Canyon in Cerocahui, into the canyon and back to the lodge. We started at 7,000 feet. We would be going twelve miles. Beautiful vistas. However, the trails were very rocky and the riverbeds very dry. We came across mountain pools which were a welcoming sight. It was hot and dry so Matt and I decided to take a plunge. Talk about shrinkage. The water was freezing. We could only stay in for a minute, it was that cold. However, there is nothing better than a splash in a mountain pool on a hot day to get refreshed. Up and down the valleys was difficult at times. In the end it was a nice day of hiking.

Getting back to the lodge all hot, dusty and thirsty, I ordered a round of cervezas. They were icy cold. We found out we were the only guests in the lodge. Matt and I played Scrabble-Spanish Scrabble. We found tiles of LL, CH, RR, and no tiles of K or W.

When Matt and I discussed what we wanted to do and see, we came to the conclusion- wherever and whatever. We planned an itinerary. It did not matter if we stuck to it or not. The next day we were to catch the train north to Divisadero. At first we were going to Creel but decided to spend a day in Divisadero due to the beauty of the place we saw on the way down. However, it didn't matter what we planned. Getting to the train, the next day, we asked the station clerk when the train north would be coming. He said "no, hoy". Not today. No train today. We did not want to stay another day in this dusty, dry town. So we said what the hell and took the next train south to El Fuerta, the other end of the Copper Canyon. All we would do was spend the night, then hop the train the next morning to Creel. We would have to pass on Divisadero. It can be a bummer to waste two days riding a train. However, that's what adventure travel is all about. Matt's a good travel companion. He realizes no matter what happens, the idea is that we are here, wherever that may be. We passed time on the train playing cribbage. Stopped again in Divisadero for fifteen minutes. This time we did some craft shopping. Bought some food and as we were paying, the train started pulling away. Running after the moving train, we grabbed the outside railing and hoisted ourselves up.

About 3:30 that afternoon we made it to the backpacker's haven, the town of Creel. From here, there are numerous side trips you can take. We stayed at Casa de Margrita's, the backpacker's standby. Dorm beds cost $6 or a room with two beds and a shower for $20, which Matt and I shared. The cost also came with breakfast and dinner. Don't get excited. It was far from a gourmet feast. However, the travel talk with all the travelers is always worth the price of admission.

We only had a day to spend so we decided to take a hike into the canyon to a hot spring at the bottom of the canyon. It was a very rocky trail being we were still in the dry season. Footing was not easy. Upon reaching bottom, we found paradise. Pools of warm water where we swam. Waterfalls and rock slides made for added fun. Ate some lunch and headed back. This was not easy for me. The steep climb with the rocky paths made for very slow going. At times like these I wonder why I just don't take a trip to lay on the beach and do nothing else.

The night was wonderful as the backpackers took over a small bar. All the adventure tales came out. Back home I am unable to tell my tales. My friends cannot understand this type of adventure travel that I do. They may appear interested, but I know they are not. Therefore, as any adventure traveler knows, shared talks with other backpackers is always exciting. I made an impression on a young traveler when he found out I crossed the Darien Gap.

Before leaving the next day, we sent a fax back to our workplace:

En Jaula (in jail)

Vemir pesos (send money)

Muchos pesos (a lot of money)

Mas Rapido (hurry)

Back at the hostel, we packed, hugged our good-byes and caught the bus to Chihuahua. Nothing exciting on the bus until some screwball got on with his accordion to "entertain."

Being the last night of our adventure trip, I stay at a nice hotel. It's my treat to myself. I also have a good dinner out. A mushroom fillet steak with potato and wine did the trick. Matt and I relived the trip. I told him what a great traveling companion he was and hoped he would lead a life of adventure, not just one of existing.

The trip was over. Just needed to fly home. However, I told Matt, this is where the adventure after the adventure usually comes. Trying to get home.

Up at six. We showered, finished packing, had a continental breakfast, took a taxi to the airport, checked in for our flight. Everything is going smoothly. Plane is to leave at 9:55am to Hermosilla, then to Phoenix, onward to Minneapolis. Looking at the clock, it is 9:30, then 9:40, now 9:55. We're still sitting in the waiting area and I don't see a plane to board. I get up to see the gate agent. There are six other passengers inquiring as to what is going on. There were no announcements. The Spanish started flying left and right and I got a sense of what I'm hearing. No plane. After getting the situation interpreted, we would catch Aero Mexico at 2:30 to Hermosillo, getting in to Phoenix at 4:30. However, our Northwest flight from Phoenix leaves at 4:00. I said to myself, the adventure after the adventure. Here I go again. We went to the Aero Mexico counter to see what they would do for us. They said they would get me to Phoenix. I said I didn't care about Phoenix, I wanted to get to Minneapolis. This took some doing. The agent worked on it for twenty minutes when he looked up at us and said, "Leave right now for immigration. Hurry!" We ran through the airport to get to customs. Got checked out. Ran back through security. An agent told us to catch that plane. We had no idea where we were going. I saw a small prop plane that we were to board. Looking at the tickets, we were going to El Paso. In El Paso, America West to Phoenix, and then America West to Minneapolis. In all, it would be a difference of ten minutes from our original arrival time on Northwest. As usual, everything worked out fine.

Conclusion

▼

FINAL THOUGHTS BUT NOT THE FINAL TRIP

People ask me what trip I like the most. Fortunately, there is no answer to this question. Each trip was unique in its own way and each was a memorable experience. Hitchhiking and staying in youth hostels offered an inexpensive, carefree, wild way to travel. We never knew where we might spend the night. It all depended on the rides we received that day. We weren't looking to see any particular sights or get to any place special. I'll never forget Garth and Gurley who offered us a place to sleep and a meal. Also, the manure truck that we were in only to be let out at a crossroads in the middle of nowhere. Nothing to do but roll down the embankment and sleep out among the stars. Not a care in the world. We were having fun. Hitchhiking one year to Montreal and the following year to Banff. We saw Canada the best way possible, from the road. Camping in a youth hostel at the base of a mountain, along a stream while a backpacker played his guitar.

What can be said about my first solo adventure to the biggest zoo in the world. Only it's not a zoo. It's a place where the animals roam freely and we had to be in a protected vehicle. We had to be in a "cage". The awesome beauty of East Africa with its animals, mountains, and jungles. I was awed every minute at my surroundings. The friendships of the group with a communication that has lasted over twenty years. Yes, I can watch all the nature shows on television but to actually be in East Africa is unmatchable to sitting in a chair in front of the tube.

Overcoming the challenge of Mt. Kilimanjaro was a feat I'll always remember. Yes, I got a little cold up at 15,520 ft. but this was so minute to the magnificence of the total climb. I look back at my achievement with pride.

Canoeing in the Everglades was my first major self guided canoe trip. Sure, it was not some massive expedition exploring the waterways of the northern tundra, but it sure beat the little canoe overnights on the local Minnesota rivers. I had to plan gear and food for eight days out. I had to study currents and tides. Where else could you be quietly paddling under a Florida sun rounding a bend in the waterway and come upon an alligator basking in the sun? The scenery and serenity of the Everglades along with a bond between my cousin and I that will last a lifetime. Hopefully, he'll relive a like experience with his son.

Peru offered a variety of mysteries and challenges. Learning that what can go wrong actually can occur was a lesson in being better prepared the next time out. Realize that events may not go as planned but in the end usually work out satisfactory. Where else can you see such a bizarre sight as the Nazca lines or the way of life of the Peruvian Indians living on the reed island on Lake Titicaca. Overcoming a scare of altitude sickness was not especially pleasant. However, these setbacks are offset by the magnificence of other aspects of the trip like the Inca ruins culminating with the hike on the Inca trail to one of the eight wonders of the world-Machu Pichu. Knowing when a change in plans is warranted due to a rebel uprising. Always, better safe than sorry.

Thailand was a study of culture. Hiking to a hilltribe village and living among a primitive people. Seeing a different way of life than what I am used to. Learning the ways of the drug, opium, and what a part the drug plays on these people. Enjoying the escapades with my Australian buddies of the Chaing Rae night life. This region of Thailand, Malaysia, Indonesia, and now Vietnam are a backpacker's paradise. Wonderful sights, exciting challenges, all at very inexpensive costs. The cultural differences, ways of everyday life, the friendliness of the people will always be remembered with a smile. Never once, did I feel in danger from my surroundings. Never once did I seem out of place just because I was different.

Burrowing through the jungles of the Darien was truly my most challenging trip. Yes, this was an adventure for the working stiff that made the everyday nine to five work day a vacation. What I endured daring the Darien will be my personal success of challenging myself to never having to look back and say I wish I did that (whatever that may be)when I was younger. The Darien Gap trip will probably be the hardest adventure of all. I became, Jungle Jay, after this trip.

I've been to Costa Rica on two different occasions. The first was when I wanted to do an adventure in a foreign country but only had a week's time to take a trip. Not wanting to waste full days traveling overseas due to lack of vacation time, I chose to go river rafting in Costa Rica. The second time I went was to be on my own with a friend to just bum around. I was to meet Erin at the Northwest Airlines counter at five thirty in the morning. As I was checking in at the gate, the phone rang. The gate agent answered the phone, looked at me, looked at the phone and looked at me again. She then said with a bewildered look that the phone was for me. It was a message from Erin that she was sick and not able to make the flight. The gate agent asked if I still wanted to go. My answer took no thinking at all and away I went. It turned out to be kind of interesting doing a solo trip. I was able to meet people so it didn't really bother me that Erin was unable to go. I traveled for a week which included a half day of river rafting and a visit to the Arenal Volcano. After all this, I headed to the town of Dominical. I met my brother and sister-in-law. They had bought a house in the mountains overlooking the ocean. I was staying at a cabana looking after the place while the owner was out of town. I got a feeling for what it was like to live there. A lot of gringos are moving to this area to enjoy a slow way of life. I made an offer on a mountain lot but my offer was not accepted. The Realtor wanted me to work with her selling real estate and setting up an adventure travel agency. This was tempting but was not going to be a reality for me. I wasn't ready to make this kind of adjustment.

Borneo was a treat. Just the name, Borneo, speaks of wonder. A small group of just five, traveled back in time. The encounter with the Dyak River people and living with them was an unimaginable experience. Seeing the lush jungle atmosphere and at the same time, the destruction of the rain forest by Japanese interests. No one can imagine what beauty is being destroyed. The destruction of a rainforest is forever. It can never be rebuilt. A way of life, a land, a people, will be no more without the rainforest.

I added the final chapters of time shares and local adventures to show that you don't have to travel with a backpack through a jungle or to the ends of the earth to have an adventure. You don't have to spend a lot of money to have an adventure. You don't have to be some super hero to be able to achieve success with a trip. Even with an impairment of some kind still enables one to have an adventure. There are outfitters and organizations for any ability and any adventure.

I can only share what I have been able to enjoy. I have learned about countries, people and cultures. The differences between people and cultures makes for a grand and exciting world. What fun would it be to travel half way around the world and encounter me? A culture the same as me. A way of life the same as me. Beliefs the same as me.

What is your thought of that encounter? My thought is of a boring world. Luckily, this is not the case. It's a wonderful exciting world, with so much to see and learn. So next time you want to take a vacation, take a trip instead. Have yourself an adventure. Live your life as an adventure, not an existence.

Printed in the United States
57573LVS00005BA/385-411